AI Guardian Angel Bots for Deep AI Trustworthiness

Practical Advances in Artificial Intelligence (AI) and Machine Learning

Dr. Lance B. Eliot, MBA, PhD

Disclaimer: This book is presented solely for educational and entertainment purposes. The author and publisher are not offering it as legal, accounting, or other professional services advice. The author and publisher make no representations or warranties of any kind and assume no liabilities of any kind with respect to the accuracy or completeness of the contents and specifically disclaim any implied warranties of merchantability or fitness of use for a particular purpose. Neither the author nor the publisher shall be held liable or responsible to any person or entity with respect to any loss or incidental or consequential damages caused, or alleged to have been caused, directly or indirectly, by the information or programs contained herein. Every company is different and the advice and strategies contained herein may not be suitable for your situation.

DEDICATION

To my wonderful daughter, Lauren, and my wonderful son, Michael.

Forest fortuna adiuvat (from the Latin; good fortune favors the brave).

CONTENTS

Lance B. Eliot

ACKNOWLEDGMENTS

I have been the beneficiary of advice and counsel by many friends, colleagues, family, investors, and many others. I want to thank everyone that has aided me throughout my career. I write from the heart and the head, having experienced first-hand what it means to have others around you that support you during the good times and the tough times.

To Warren Bennis, one of my doctoral advisors and ultimately a colleague, I offer my deepest thanks and appreciation, especially for his calm and insightful wisdom and support.

To Mark Stevens and his generous efforts toward funding and supporting the USC Stevens Center for Innovation.

To Lloyd Greif and the USC Lloyd Greif Center for Entrepreneurial Studies for their ongoing encouragement of founders and entrepreneurs.

To Peter Drucker, William Wang, Aaron Levie, Peter Kim, Jon Kraft, Cindy Crawford, Jenny Ming, Steve Milligan, Chis Underwood, Frank Gehry, and Colonel Sanders, Buzz Aldrin, Steve Forbes, Bill Thompson, Dave Dillon, Alan Fuerstman, Larry Ellison, Jim Sinegal, John Sperling, Mark Stevenson, Anand Nallathambi, Thomas Barrack, Jr., and many other innovators and leaders that I have met and gained mightily from doing so.

Thanks to Ed Trainor, Kevin Anderson, James Hickey, Wendell Jones, Ken Harris, DuWayne Peterson, Mike Brown, Jim Thornton, Abhi Beniwal, Al Biland, John Nomura, and many others for their unwavering support during my career.

And most of all thanks as always to Lauren and Michael, for their ongoing support and for having seen me writing and heard much of this material during the many months involved in writing it. To their patience and willingness to listen.

Lance B. Eliot

INTRODUCTION

This is a book about Artificial Intelligence (AI). I will be covering various technical aspects of AI, along with also encompassing business aspects, and blend the two together at times.

To aid you, the reader, whether you are oriented toward business interests or perhaps oriented instead toward more technical interests, I have tried to explain any arcane terminology whenever I make use of it in the book. I hope to make this book readily readable for anyone generally interested in the specific topic being discussed.

We will be discussing AI Guardian Angel Bots and Deep AI. And trust, and trustworthiness. Doing so for practical, important, and vital reasons.

The specific topic is a bit of a mouthful, and includes some new phrases, so allow me a moment to elaborate on what this book is exactly about. You might have noticed that the title of the book includes the phrase "Deep AI" and so I would like to start there and offer some thoughts on what the phrase means.

You might find first of idle interest that I have been a long-time active participant and contributor to the field of AI, having started during the heyday of AI during the 1980's. I was a professor and researcher of AI. At one point, I started and ran one of the first research labs on AI in business. For several years, I was called the "AI insider" and wrote a regular monthly column about the latest trends in AI. I did research studies on AI, served on editorial boards for AI related journals, etc.

I even launched what became a highly successful consulting business, which was born via the use of AI for business. I admit that I have a bit of a bias toward the application of AI, more so than the more obtuse basic research of AI. That being said, I welcome and encourage the basic or foundational AI research and find it immensely powerful and important.

We are now seeing a resurgence of AI. There was an AI Winter, as some would call it, and now, as the snow melts, a new AI Spring is emerging. Those of us that have continued to toil away in AI, doing so while the limelight no longer shined, find this AI Spring quite exciting and a heartwarming reminder that we are on the right path.

Every day, you likely have seen a new announcement about some advancement in AI and how it will change business and society. A recent featured article in *Fortune* magazine emphasized that Deep AI is changing how we live, and furthermore that venture capitalists now are insisting that any tech startup should make use of AI (see the *Fortune* article entitled "Why Deep Learning is Suddenly Changing Your Life"). This is another sign, perhaps a billboard sized sign, emphasizing the rebirth of AI.

AI, MACHINE LEARNING, DEEP AI

AI is defined variously by many authors and pundits. I will avoid getting into a prolonged debate herein, and simply say that the field of AI is about being able to create and field automated systems that embody intelligent behavior and characteristics. That's my quick but sufficient definition.

You might contrast Artificial Intelligence to biological-based intelligence, in that we as humans (and other animals) showcase intelligent behavior, and for which it is attributed to the cognitive capabilities of our brains. There is a tremendous amount of research taking place to crack the mystery of how intelligent behavior arises out of our brains (some call our brains "wetware" to contrast it to conventional automation which is usually known as "hardware"). Right now, we mainly study the plumbing and wiring of the true brain, examining neurons, synapses, chemical interchanges, and the like, in the hopes of being able to discern how it magically seems to give rise to what we call intelligence.

AI is an umbrella term, covering all the ways in which we might be able to make intelligent systems. This includes for example Natural Language Processing (NLP). NLP advancements have been probably the most visible of all AI aspects to the everyday world. Via Siri and Alexa, we witness the AI systems for NLP, which parse verbal utterances, identify words, try to figure out the semantics of sentences, and then get toward the meaning of what has been said.

Machine learning is considered another branch under the AI umbrella. It generally refers to the notion that an intelligent system should presumably be able to learn, since humans and other animals that have intelligence seem to be able to learn. If we want to create intelligent systems in automation, they would need to have a capacity to learn, though what it means to "learn" something is still open to discussion and further research.

One of the most popular ways nowadays to have automation that appears to be able to learn involves the use of **Artificial Neural Networks** (ANN). ANN's are akin to a simulation, kind of, about what we believe is happening in the brain. There are an estimated 100 billion or more neurons in the actual brain, and we are not yet near being able to create a workable, functionally equivalent version of a brain in automation that well simulates that number of neurons along with their interconnections, and gives rise to intelligent behavior on the scale of the human brain.

Some ANN researchers try to strictly abide by the same aspects of what we believe is occurring in the wetware brain, while others don't feel that we need to necessarily abide by how the human brain works per se. Plus, since there are still so many open questions about the inner workings of the brain, if ANN waited until all secrets of the human brain were revealed we might not make progress in ANN for as yet many years to come.

Deep Learning is a relatively new phrase that some would say is Machine Learning taken to a deeper degree of capability. Whereas in the prior AI Spring we might have had artificial neural networks with just a few layers and few dozens of neurons, the latest versions go far beyond those limits. During the years since the last elation about AI, advances in hardware miniaturization, the reduction in cost of such hardware, and improvements in the software, have led to the now ability to more readily create and field these systems.

We also need to look at the advances in sensory devices too. The amount of sensory devices that goes into a self-driving car would have been so massive in size and so costly that it would have been quite difficult to put together a car that could do what today's self-driving cars do. You would have needed a refrigerator sized processing box tied to the roof of the car, and the cameras and radar devices would have made the car look like one of those enormous tractor-trailer trucks you see on the highways.

Deep AI, which is not yet a popularized term, but one that I find handy to use, refers to going more deeply into all of the umbrella aspects of AI, including and foremost Machine Learning, which begat Deep Learning. In this book, I have chosen to use Deep AI as a convenient label for anything that is an AI-based system that is attempting to exhibit intelligent or intelligent-like behavior, and for which uses today's modern approaches to do so (that's where the "deep" part of Deep AI comes to play).

From my view, if I said "Deep Learning" rather than Deep AI in this book, it would imply that I am only interested in the particular aspects of AI systems that embody learning capabilities. It is why I am preferring to use the "Deep AI" because I want to ensure that you know that I am going wider than that.

I realize that some AI purists won't like my using Deep AI in this manner, or might disagree with the name entirely. I ask that you just go with the flow, and it really won't make a difference here, since I could have called it a rose, as long as I defined what I meant by a rose. Well, and as long as you, the reader, weren't thrown off by seeing the word "rose" throughout this book.

DEEP AI AND BORROWING FROM ASIMOV

Hopefully, you are now comfortable that when I refer to Deep AI that I am discussing intelligent-like systems that make use of modern day "deep" AI capabilities.

We are gradually going to see Deep AI in all sorts of ways around us. The self-driving car is the most eye catching. You can also expect to see it in your smart toaster, in your smart refrigerator, at your local fast food cookery, etc. The Internet of Things (IoT) will be composed of both "dumb" devices and "smart" devices, whereby the so-called "smart" devices will have some variant of Deep AI embedded in them.

I want to now bring up a topic that at first glance might seem science fiction oriented, and for which I don't want to have you believe that I am going on a wayward tangent. You will get my drift pretty quickly, so hang in there, as what I am about to do is explain why this book and the topic of this book is actually a very serious topic, and one that has not only societal repercussions but also presents great business opportunities (and threats).

You might be aware that a famous science fiction writer, Issac Asimov, wrote about robots and in his 1942 story entitled "Runaround" he postulated three laws about robots. These laws about robots have been used frequently in many of our most popular science fiction movies, TV shows, and in many other contexts. Think of Star Wars and Star Trek, and I assure you that you've seen, heard, or otherwise been shown the three laws.

I am going to focus on the first of the three laws, and it says this:

"A robot may not injure a human being or, through inaction, allow a human being to come to harm."

I would like to slightly alter it, in order to fit to our purposes here:

A Deep AI system may not injure a human being or, through inaction, allow a human being to come to harm.

I replaced the word "robot" with the phrase "Deep AI" and did so because when you see the word "robot" in his sentence, you probably right away imagined some clunky metallic creature walking around with squeaky arms and legs.

I want to get you away from that image, since otherwise Asimov's originally written law might drag you back into that wild imagery. The Deep AI that we are referring to here is something that you might not ever actually see with your own eyes. For example, with a self-driving car, the Deep AI is running on computer processors that are hidden inside the body of the car. You don't see a robot at the wheel of the car.

We are now at a juncture then of considering the modified version of the first law. Let's take a look at it again:

A Deep AI system may not injure a human being or, through inaction, allow a human being to come to harm.

I am saying that wherever Deep AI is put into use, whether in your smart toaster or in your self-driving car, it should be a crucial dictum that it will not injure you, nor others. This avoidance of harming you, or others, should be by inherent design and intent. It should also encompass the possibility of inaction, as Asimov so cleverly included.

For example, let's consider a self-driving car. The Deep AI of the self-driving car should be able to drive the car, safely, since it is acting on your behalf, and avoid injuring or harming you. Suppose your self-driving car opted to run a red light and then another car crashed into you, this would be a violation of the dictum.

Suppose that the self-driving car was driving along and was in the middle of an intersection when a human-driven car ran a red light. If the Deep AI of the self-driving car takes no action to avoid the oncoming human-driven car, and allows by default the crash into you, and you are injured, this is again a violation of the dictum (since inaction counts in the dictum).

DEEP AI AND TRUST

Let's now move away from science fiction and into the realm of the real-world. Those self-driving car examples that I just mentioned could both be true. We are going to have self-driving cars that will run a red light and cause an injury. How can I be so sure of this?

The complexities of the Deep AI in the self-driving cars and the aspects of being able to cover all possible combinations of ways that an injury or harm can result is just so enormous that we cannot be fully assured of what a self-driving car will do in all cases. Maybe the self-driving car was trying to avoid an even worse predicted accident by not driving into the intersection. Or, maybe the self-driving car suffered a hardware malfunction, which manifested at a moment in time that led the self-driving car to go into the intersection. And so on.

There will be tremendous efforts by the developers of these Deep AI systems to try and programmatically avoid harmful results. But, if you are thinking that these Deep AI systems will be "perfect" and never will a single instance arise of harm to humans, you had better pinch yourself because you aren't living in the real-world.

Does the aspect that the Deep AI systems are going to at some points involve harm to humans mean that we should not be using them? I don't want to again get bogged down in such perhaps morality kinds of questions here. I'll just point out that one could say that we should not be using conventional cars at all since there is the chance of injury or death to humans by the use of cars. And by the use of planes. And by the use of bicycles (you might like to know that according to Federal government figures, Florida recorded an annual average of about 5.7 cyclist deaths per million residents last year).

Ethicists will be steaming at that comparison, so let me help their side of this to indicate that when unleashing technology onto the marketplace, those that do so presumably will have both a moral and legal obligation to consider safety. And, if the avoid doing so, or inadequately do so, there should and likely will be consequences.

Anyway, I think it is pretty clear that the train is moving forward on the adoption of Deep AI. It is probably going to get messy as Deep AI becomes more pervasive and the topic of safety looms more prominently in the media. A minor incident here or there, right now, does not set off any alarm bells. Once the per capita interaction with Deep AI goes through the roof, the number of harming instances and the clamor to do something about them is going to ring, I assure you.

Consumers will lose whatever trust they had in Deep AI. Right now, consumers don't know much about what it is. They also don't interact much with it. For now, most consumers are on-the-fence about trusting Deep AI. As we will explore in the next chapter, there are tiny pockets of consumers that currently interact with variations of Deep AI, but for various reasons that we'll see, their trust is currently high, but this should not be extrapolated to all consumers.

A GUARDIAN ANGEL ON YOUR SIDE

If we all had a guardian angel, looking over our shoulders, we would be much safer. Imagine that you could somehow conjure up a guardian angel. Wouldn't that be nifty!

This book is about your being able to do just that. Not in a mystical way. I am referring instead to having a Bot that would serve as your guardian angel. You have probably heard about Bots. If you are using Facebook messenger, which according to Facebook they claim that about 900 million people a month interact with Facebook messenger, you have likely encountered a Bot. The most popular variants of Bots right now is the Chat Bot.

A Chat Bot comes to play in the middle of your texting with a friend, let's say. You have entered the word "pizza" into your text message to your friend. Facebook, scanning the text of your text messages, then launches a Chat Bot that is provided by Dominos. The Dominos bot asks you if you want to order a large pizza with anchovies. It does this because it already "knows" that you like anchovies on your pizza.

I suppose you might say that the Dominos chat bot was acting like a "Guardian Angel" because it was kind of looking over your shoulder and realized you were hungry for pizza. I am not going to accept that quite as a guardian angel of the nature that I am referring to in this book.

I am referring to a Guardian Angel that seeks to keep you out of harm's way. And, in particular, out of harm's way when you are dependent upon Deep AI.

In short, there is a new breed of AI-technology that I am calling the "AI Guardian Angel Bot" which would be looking over your shoulder on your behalf when you are dependent upon Deep AI, and act in your best interests to try and ensure that the Deep AI does not lead you into harm.

AI GUARDIAN ANGEL BOTS

I want you to be aware that this is a relatively new aspect, and so you won't find much that has been written or researched on the topic directly. It is so new that even the name for it is still being established, somewhat by osmosis.

Names I've heard include:

- o   AI Guardian
- o   AI Watchdog
- o   AI Sentinel
- o   AI Surveilling
- o   AI Safeguard
- o   AI Oversight

I am not going to argue which name is best for this line of products and research. I have opted to use the moniker of "AI Guardian Angels" because I think it seems more expressive than saying "AI Guardian" and I also have co-joined the word "Bots" so as to make it clearer that this is not some magical thing.

If I told you that there were these "AI Guardian Angels" you might look up at the sky and expect to see winged creatures. Instead, if I say "AI Guardian Angel Bots" it then gets you into thinking about bots overall, like Chat Bots, and so you then would consider that having a certain kind of bot that was acting as an AI Guardian Angel seems to be a reasonable proposition, I believe.

One academic article that I think you might find interesting on the topic of the AI oversight aspects is this one from the Communications of the ACM entitled "Designing AI Systems that Obey Our Laws and Values" and was written by Amitai Etzioni, Professor of Sociology at GWU, and Oren Etzioni, CEO of the Allen Institute for AI and a Professor at the University of Washington.

Their article provides a broad view of the societal and ethics concerns about Deep AI systems, and the role of the AI Guardian or AI Oversight system. Years ago, I served on the editorial board of the Communications of the ACM, and I still to this day appreciate their willingness and determination to consider not just technical aspects of computer science but to also provide a forum for looking at the social implications too.

For this herein book, I am focusing more so on the business and technical aspects of Deep AI and the AI Guardian Angel bots, but do want you to consider reading the piece by Etzioni and Etzioni which is an important call to thought and action for the future of Deep AI and our society.

WHAT THIS BOOK PROVIDES

What does this book provide to you? It introduces the notion of AI Guardian Angel bots, and presents a technical and business basis for them. The book provides an indication of how the AI Guardian Angel bots might be assessed and utilized.

It provides an indication of the technical aspects such as the API's (Application Programming Interface) and software design patterns associated with them, and how they will interact with Deep AI.

Throughout, I use the self-driving car as an example, and an example involving a robot cleaning a home. This will make the concepts and approaches described here more understandable and reachable.

Let's do a quick tour of the book.

In Chapter 1, we will explore the meaning of "trust" and how it applies to Deep AI, including consumer perception and willingness to use Deep AI. This will set the stage for further justifying the AI Guardian Angel bot as a means of boosting trust by consumers of Deep AI, plus genuinely helping to further protect people.

In Chapter 2, we look at some of the practical aspects of AI Guardian Angel bots, including how they will emerge on a market time-lag basis, following closely on the heels of the advent of Deep AI.

In Chapter 3, I provide a set of foundational API's for the interplay of Deep AI and the AI Guardian Angel bots.

In Chapter 4 and Chapter 5, I explore the ecosystem of AI Guardian Angel bots that will emerge over time, along with the rise of ratings and safety levels for assessing AI Guardian Angel bots.

In Chapter 6, there are some Deep AI "failure modes" that researchers are trying to mitigate or overcome. I walk through a means by which AI Guardian Angel bots can help with this pursuit.

In Chapter 7, I look at the role of multiple agents, such that we might have a Deep AI system interacting with more than one AI Guardian Angel bot.

In Chapter 8, we consider the importance of Belief Systems that are at the underpinning of sophisticated Deep AI and also in AI Guardian Angel bots.

In Chapter 9, we cover some key design patterns for AI Guardian Angel bots. This might spark progress on the creation and fielding of AI Guardian Angel bots.

WHY THIS BOOK

I wrote this book to try and establish that Deep AI will likely face a crisis of trust, and that besides trying to avoid or lessen the crisis generally, we can make use of AI Guardian Angel bots in that quest.

For business leaders considering the adoption of Deep AI into their products and services, I hope that this book will enlighten you as to the risks involved and ways in which you should be strategizing about how to deal with those risks.

For entrepreneurs, startups and other businesses that want to enter into the AI Guardian Angel bot market that will emerge, I hope this book sparks your interest in doing so, and provides some sense of what might be prudent to pursue.

For researchers that study AI, I hope this book spurs your interest in the risks and safety issues of Deep AI, and also nudges you toward conducting research on AI Guardian Angel bots.

For students in computer science or related disciplines, I hope this book will provide you with interesting and new ideas and material, for which you might conduct research or provide some career direction insights for you.

For AI companies and high-tech companies pursuing AI, this book will hopefully keep your eye on the safety aspects of Deep AI and ensure that you realize that investments in the safety aspects will have their reward, which might not seem to be the case in the short-term but will be so in the long-term.

For all readers, I hope that you will find the material in this book to be stimulating. Some of it will be repetitive of things you already know. But I am pretty sure that you'll also find various eureka moments whereby you'll discover a new technique or approach that you had not earlier thought of. I am also betting that there will be material that forces you to rethink some of your current practices.

I am not saying you will suddenly have an epiphany and change what you are doing. I do think though that you will reconsider or perhaps revisit what you are doing.

For anyone choosing to use this book for teaching purposes, please take a look at my suggestions for doing so, as described in the Appendix. I have found the material handy in courses that I have taught, and likewise other faculty have told me that they have found the material handy, in some cases as extended readings and in other instances as a core part of their course (depending on the nature of the class).

In my writing for this book, I have tried carefully to blend both the practitioner and the academic styles of writing. It is not as dense as is typical academic journal writing, but at the same time offers depth by going into the nuances and trade-offs of various practices.

The word "deep" is in vogue today, meaning getting deeply into a subject or topic, and so is the word "unpack" which means to tease out the underlying aspects of a subject or topic. I have sought to offer material that addresses an issue or topic by going relatively deeply into it and make sure that it is well unpacked.

Finally, in any book about AI, it is difficult to use our everyday words without having some of them be misinterpreted. Specifically, it is easy to anthropomorphize AI. When I say that an AI system "knows" something, I do not want you to construe that the AI system has sentience and "knows" in the same way that humans do. They aren't that way, as yet. I have tried to use quotes around such words from time-to-time to emphasize that the words I am using should not be misinterpreted to ascribe true human intelligence to the AI systems that we know of today. If I used quotes around all such words, the book would be very difficult to read, and so I am doing so judiciously. Please keep that in mind as you read the material, thanks.

Lance B. Eliot

CHAPTER 1

ISSUES OF TRUST ABOUT DEEP AI

CHAPTER 1

ISSUES OF TRUST ABOUT DEEP AI

PREFACE

In this chapter, I tackle an increasingly worrisome topic, namely the advent of Deep AI and the trust or lack of trust that people are willing to put toward using Deep AI.

Are you willing today to get into a self-driving car, one that is completely and exclusively controlled by Deep AI? When I say get into such a self-driving car, I am saying that you would let it navigate the toughest of driving situations, involving other cars nearby, traffic snarls, nutty car drivers swerving toward you, drunk drivers on the road, potholes in the road, bridges that are out, during a severe lightning and rain storm, and so on.

Recent surveys reveal that most consumers have very serious doubts about self-driving cars. Nearly 80% in a recent poll by Kelly Blue Book said that they would always want the option to take over the wheel of the car. A hefty 64% said they could not envision Deep AI (an automated system) being fully in control of their car. Plainly, right now, consumers don't trust Deep AI, at least for car driving. We will need to see what other areas that Deep AI gets immersed into and whether consumers will be willing to trust Deep AI in this circumstances.

It is useful to understand what it means to say that someone "trusts" someone else or something. We explore the nature of trust in this chapter, and also how it impacts Deep AI, plus what can be done about it.

———

CHAPTER 1:

ISSUES OF TRUST
ABOUT DEEP AI

This chapter is about trust. A well-known "tech expert" recently spoke publicly about trust and technology – it was the CEO of Microsoft and he stated that with any technology, including and particularly naming AI, building trust with people and organizations about using the technology is one of the "pressing issues of our times" (as reported in the WSJ).

If we build and field systems with Deep AI, will people use them? Some take it as an axiom that if we build it, they will come. But, this is a rather simplistic view and one that seems to ignore the trust issue. The better mousetrap, if not trustworthy, will not likely succeed in the market. Indeed, by being "better" we should encompass that the system not only serves its stated purpose, but does so in a manner that creates and imbues trust, such that it will continue to be used over time.

What does it mean to build trust? Our everyday use of the word trust has a wide variety of meanings. It is worthwhile to take a moment and explore the nature of "trust" and see how it is embodied in the real-world. I will start with the notion of trust being a form of encapsulated interest (a theory that some like and some don't; see Russell Hardin's work for a detailed exploration of this line of thought). See Figure 1.

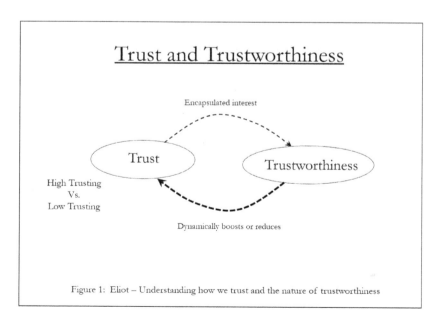

Figure 1: Eliot – Understanding how we trust and the nature of trustworthiness

TRUST AND TRUSTWORTHINESS

We will consider trust to be something that we store within us. It is a cognitive aspect that we often take for granted. I trust my children. Okay, that seems to make sense, but what does it mean? It means that within my mind, I believe that they are trustworthy. Trustworthiness is integral to trust, and serves as our means to gauge how much or how little trust we want to apply to others.

Take a look again at Figure 1. As shown, we have Trust, which is being fed by Trustworthiness. The trustworthiness of someone or something will modify my level of trust, increasing or decreasing it. This is dynamic. It is happening continuously. One moment my trust level for someone might be high, and the next moment low.

My trust in my children is based upon my expectations of their behavior and their motivations toward me. It is my belief of their encapsulated interest about me. I believe that they are motivated to try and do what's good or best for me. They have an interest in my well-being. Let's say we go hiking in the mountains. We have reached a narrow path along the edge of a cliff. My daughter steps ahead of me, looks back, and tells me that I should follow her. Do I trust her?

I might. I might have a high level of trust in her, believing that she has an encapsulated interest that is sincere and persistent, and I can rely upon her to be thinking of my safety. She has shown herself to be trustworthy over time, building up a large and persistent reservoir of trust within me. So, I step onto the path.

If the person ahead of me was a complete stranger, rather than my daughter, and if they turned to tell me it was safe, I would have presumably almost none of a trust reservoir for this person. They have not demonstrated to me trustworthiness over time, and so my trust level for them is presumably low. Suppose though it was a hired guide for the trip, an expert in hiking, I might have a high level of trust in what the guide says.

There are some that start an encounter with others and make an assumption of a high level of trust, while there are others that start with a low level of trust (or perhaps something in-between).

I say this to emphasize that the nature of how trust is treated by a particular person is shaped around their own particular beliefs and assumptions about the world. Suppose you have grown-up in an environment where you learned to not trust anyone, you would presumably always have a starting level of low trust for anyone you meet anew.

Maybe instead you grew up in a manner believing that everyone is worth trusting until they disprove that trust. For you, you always grant a stranger a high level of trust, and watch to see how they act to then decide which direction the trust level about them should go. You might have the proverbial "trust, but verify" kind of perspective, meaning that you grant others high levels of trust and then subtract if they don't validate the trust you have allotted to them.

THREE-PART TRUST RELATIONSHIP

Generally, you can think of trust as being a three-part relationship when interacting with others and undertaking a task. I am taking us to this formulation of trust because it is applicable to using technology. See Figure 2.

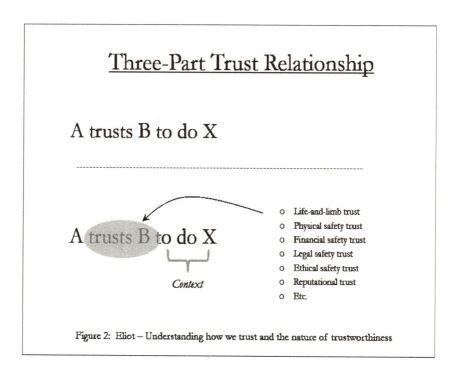

Figure 2: Eliot – Understanding how we trust and the nature of trustworthiness

As shown, we have this assertion: "A trusts B to do X" (see top of Figure 2). To clarify, when there is a person A, and they are relying upon someone else, whom we'll call B, it is for the purpose of doing something X, and we either have sufficient trust in B to undertake this or we have insufficient trust in B. Presumably, if there is insufficient trust in B to do X for us, we would try to avoid having B do this task for us.

There are a wide variety of types of trust in our trust reservoir. Take another look at Figure 2.

Not all trust is one kind or one type. There is the life-and-limb type of trust. When my daughter was on the cliff ahead of me, I might have an overall very high level of trust in her, but when it comes to a life-or-limb portion of the trust reservoir, I might not be quite as trusting. This is not to say that I somehow don't trust her at all. It just means that in circumstances involving life-and-limb, I might be not as trusting as I would be in other contexts.

Other types of trust include financial trust. A close friend approaches me and says that they have an investment in swamp land in Florida that will make a zillion dollars. I trust this friend for all sorts of things, including that we go sky diving together. But, when it comes to financial matters, my friend has always made the wild gambles. So, in this case, I politely turn down the offer of buying the swamp land. My trust in my friend remains the same as it was before. Low on financial trust, but high in other buckets of trust.

There is legal trust, meaning that I have trust as it pertains to whether the other might get me into legal trouble or not. There is ethical trust, which pertains to my ethics and whether the other might support my sense of ethical conduct. There is reputational trust, which involves that the other might support or might undermine my reputation. And so on.

A AND B CAN BE SYSTEMS LIKE DEEP AI

When I was explaining the "A trusts B to do X" it was indicated that the assertion involves person "A" trusting person "B" to do whatever "X" is. I purposely used the word *person* to make things easier to explain. Now, let me expand upon that thought.

Imagine that you are person A. I hope you like this designation. People will start referring to you as "A" and saying, "Hey, A, how you doing?" Anyway, you are trying to get your car fixed. You take it into your local car dealership. The car mechanic, person B, will fix your car. This then implies "You are trusting the car mechanic to fix your car" wherein, you are A, the car mechanic is B, and the X is your car.

Suppose instead that you are doing your taxes. You have purchased the latest version of SuperTurbo Tax, a software package for doing your taxes. In this case, you are person A, the SuperTurbo Tax package is B, and doing your taxes is X. So, you are trusting not a person per se, but trusting a software package. I mention this to point out that the "B" in the sentence of "A trusts B to do X" could be a piece of technology and not necessarily a person. We will need to keep this in mind when we get to discussing the emerging Deep AI systems, since they will be the "B" in our sentence.

I will also forewarn you that the "A" does not have to be a person either. When we get to a later chapter on belief systems of AI, I'll ask you to revisit the "A trusts B to do X" and look at the notion in the context that we might have an AI system, we'll call it A, trusting another AI system, we'll call it B, to do X.

Back to the matter at hand. We were discussing that trust is like a reservoir, and it has various portions that are shaped around trust by life-or-limb, or by financial matters, or by ethics, and so on. The level of trust can be high or low, or something in-between. Your levels of trust for others is specific to those others, and your trust levels are dynamically rising and lowering, depending upon what you are doing and what is taking place.

DISTRUST AND THE TRUST RESERVOIR

How does distrust fit into all of this? Take a look at Figure 3. We show that trustworthiness is filling the trust reservoir, meanwhile distrust will be draining it.

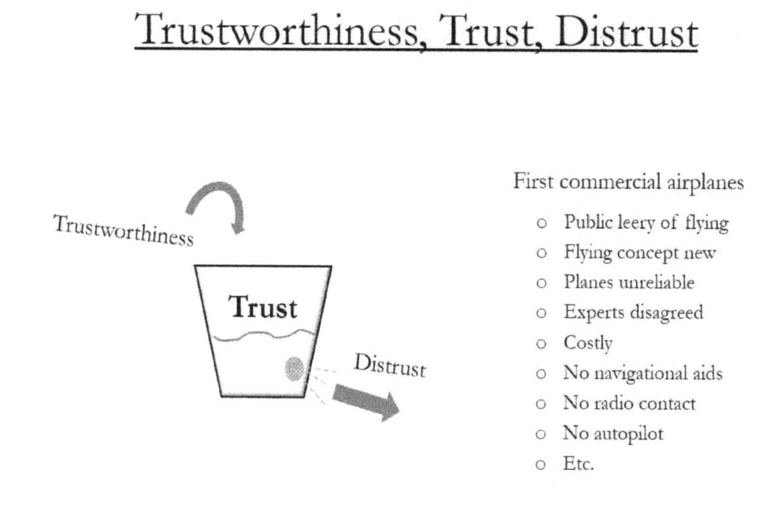

Figure 3: Eliot – Understanding how we trust and the nature of trustworthiness

You hire a guide for hiking. You at first assume they must be qualified, since they have a badge that says "Guide" and they are touting that they are an expert hiker. Follow me, says the guide, and you march along behind him. After wandering among a bunch of trees, you suddenly notice that you have seen the same tree twice. It seems like you are doubling back on your own hiking. You ask the guide about this. He says, darn, you are right, he got lost and just hoped no one else would notice.

Unless you like having a clueless hiking guide, I am betting you find him to not be as trustworthy as you at first assumed. He has now caused you to distrust him. Not entirely, since you might wave off this one mistake as a fluke. Some amount of your trust for the guide has now been drained.

TECHNOLOGY SUCH AS AIRPLANES

When commercial flights were first available, the general public pretty much avoided taking any such flights. Keep in mind that without airplanes, people had to toil in long sea voyages, or take lumbering trains that took forever, while the airplane offered a much quicker ride to your destination. Today, it is hard for us to imagine not using plane travel.

Why did people not want to fly? Take a look again at Figure 3. First, the concept of people being able to fly was quite new. Flying had been a long dream of mankind but few doubted it could ever happen. Planes were initially unreliable. They would not stay up for their intended duration. They would crash. They would not start.

Experts disagreed about whether flying was safe or not. People were confused because the experts themselves argued about the safety of flight travel. Who was right and which expert was wrong? Flying was quite costly, and so you had to ascertain whether the cost of other means of travel was more prudent for your budget. There were no navigational aids, and so the navigating of the plane would sometimes mean that the pilot would land at the wrong destination.

Why then did people not want to fly? I can answer that question in one word: Trust. People did not fly because they did not trust the technology known as airplanes. Their sense of trust was based on a variety of trustworthiness factors, such as whether the technology worked as promised (did it start, did it stay in the air), whether it was safe (instances of plane crashes, experts saying it was unsafe), and so on.

Deep AI finds itself in this same situation. It is a new technology, people aren't yet exactly sure about it, they will be hearing more and more stories about it, they aren't sure it is even possible, experts often argue over whether it is safe, etc. In short, Deep AI will face and is facing a Trust issue.

TRUST AND DEEP AI

Take a look at Figure 4. Today, there is a positive perception of the trustworthiness of Deep AI that is filling the trust bucket about Deep AI. We read stories about self-driving cars that go for millions of miles without any reported indications of destruction or deaths (we'll come back to this in the next chapter). Reporters gush about how Deep AI is going to solve many of the world's problems. So, it seems like Deep AI is trustworthy.

On the other hand, we hear about a self-driving car that crashed and injured someone, or they even died, and this heightens our distrust, draining away from the trust bucket of Deep AI.

One aspect about trust is that it often takes a long time to fill-up the bucket to higher levels, but often it is quick to drain. For example, it won't take many examples of Deep AI leading to death or destruction to undermine even a vast array of trustworthiness signals that have bombarded the market. It is the classic "one bad apple in the barrel" that could undermine Deep AI severely.

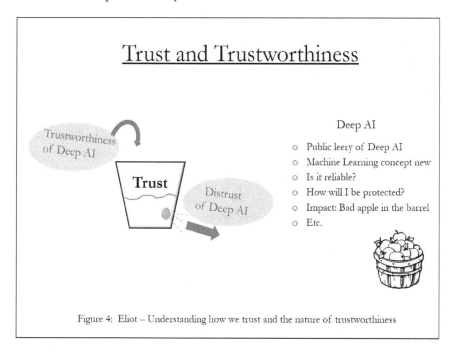

Figure 4: Eliot – Understanding how we trust and the nature of trustworthiness

FOUR-PART TRUST RELATIONSHIP

As a seasoned Deep AI developer and researcher, I certainly hope that we will continue to find ways to ensure that Deep AI systems are trustworthy. We need to be mindful of the dangers of releasing an untried Deep AI system that becomes the bad apple in the barrel. We should do whatever we can to make sure that Deep AI is as robust and bullet-proof as we can.

In the next chapter, we'll take a look at this topic and will reveal that in spite of even the most exhaustive efforts to try and make sure Deep AI is trustworthy, it is inevitable that it will still have weaknesses and leave a gap. As such, the question arises, what else can be done?

Let's expand the three-part trust relationship to find the answer to this question of what else can be done. Take a look at Figure 5. At the top of the Figure 5 is the three-part trust relationship, and below it I have expanded this to become a four-part trust relationship.

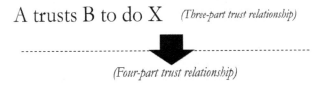

Four-Part Trust Relationship

A trusts B to do X   *(Three-part trust relationship)*

(Four-part trust relationship)

A trusts B to do X when being monitored by Y (on behalf of A)

Figure 5: Eliot – Understanding how we trust and the nature of trustworthiness

The sentence in the four-part trust relationship is this:

A trusts B to do X when being monitored by Y (on behalf of A)

Let's explore this new sentence. We have added Y to the trust relationship. Pretend for the moment that Y is a person.

For example, you are going to do your taxes, and you bought the SuperTurbo Tax package to help you do so. You use it. You finish doing your taxes. The package seems to have done all the needed tax calculations. Do you trust it? Are you willing to risk the ire of the IRS if you have somehow miscalculated your taxes?

You might decide to consult a tax expert. The tax expert does not need to do your taxes per se, since they are already done, and only needs to look them over. A kind of sanity check, as it will. The tax expert now becomes the Y in the sentence. Namely, you are person A, you trust the SuperTurbo Tax package which is B, but you have used person Y to validate B, in order to properly and legally do your taxes X.

Does hiring Y increase your trust in B? Probably not in this instance. Does this increase your trust though that the result X will be correct? Yes.

Now, let's switch up the example. You have taken your car into one of those places that can do a smog check of your car, which the DMV requires you to get done. You are A, the smog check specialist is B, and the X is the undertaking of the proper smog check of your car. Do you trust the smog check specialist to properly do the smog check of your car? Maybe yes, maybe no. The smog check place looks shady. The price they are charging is half what other places charge. The smog check specialist is on her first day of the job.

Let's suppose that the state smog inspector for your county has happened into the smog check place. He says that he is there to do an inspection, and offers to monitor the smog check specialist. The inspector says that he, the inspector, isn't going to do the smog check on your car, but will be happy to monitor the smog check specialist and even provide guidance when relevant.

What has happened now with your trust in this circumstance? I would assume that you would likely agree that your trust has gone up. You now have Y, the state authorized and official inspector, whom will be monitoring B, the smog check specialist, in order to achieve the proper smog check X. Not only will Y monitor the efforts of X, but even provide guidance when needed.

Does this make B any more trustworthy? Somewhat. We now believe that since the inspector is monitoring and guiding B, we can place a bit more trust in B. We might have preferred that B, the smog check specialist, had more training and experience and was better at the job, but, given that they aren't, having the person Y to watch over things is certainly helpful.

Notice that the state inspector has offered to specifically and directly watch over the smog check that you are having done. In that sense, the inspector is working on your behalf. I say this because if the inspector had walked in, and offered to monitor someone else's car, it wouldn't have done much good for you. You, the person A, are increasing your trust in B, the smog check specialist, because the inspector Y, is working on your behalf (A), in order to make sure that X gets done properly.

AI GUARDIAN ANGEL BOT IS THE FOURTH-PART

Have you guessed where I am walking you to? Perhaps you have. I am taking you toward the notion that the four-part trust relationship has added Y, which boosts the trust level of A. And, furthermore, the Y does not need to be a person. The Y could be a system or software.

I am calling that software or system the AI Guardian Angel Bot. It exists to be the fourth-part of the trust relationship. See Figure 6.

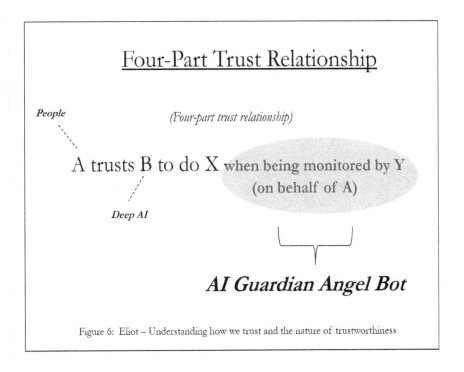

Four-Part Trust Relationship

People

(Four-part trust relationship)

A trusts B to do X when being monitored by Y (on behalf of A)

Deep AI

AI Guardian Angel Bot

Figure 6: Eliot – Understanding how we trust and the nature of trustworthiness

Now, we are ready for the final version of our four-part trust relationship sentence.

A person trusts a particular Deep AI to do X when the Deep AI is being monitored and potentially guided by an AI Guardian Angel Bot that has been devised for that specific purpose.

I have tried to keep that sentence purposely focused and not overly generalized. For example, I said that the AI Guardian Angel bot has been devised for the specific purpose. This means that not just any AI Guardian Angel bot will work for any random kind of situation. Just like the state smog check inspector can't likely help you with your taxes, each AI Guardian Angel bot will be devised for a specific purpose.

Similarly, the AI Guardian Angel bot is likely to only be able to be applicable for particular X's and particular B's. I might have one AI Guardian Angel bot that is suitable for monitoring the Deep AI of a self-driving car, but it cannot also monitor my home robot that does my house cleaning. The self-driving car is a particular type of "B" in our sentence of the person or thing doing the work, and likewise the Deep AI for the self-driving car is applicable to just the self-driving car.

It is my contention that even though we should all be striving to make Deep AI as trustworthy as possible, it alone will still have trustworthiness issues. Distrust will drain away from the trust reservoir of Deep AI. One added means to boost the trust of the Deep AI will be to augment the Deep AI with an external agent, in this case specialized software, which has the purpose of aiding to oversee the Deep AI, in the particular circumstances of whatever the Deep AI is tasked to do.

The AI Guardian Angel bot then becomes the "encapsulated interest" of being there to aid the person that is using the Deep AI. The person's trust level for the Deep AI goes up because they now have an added "expert" in their corner, fighting for them. The AI Guardian Angel bot is like that state smog inspector, bringing to the task at hand an added expert perspective, monitoring and guiding.

Not only does this boost trust by the person using the Deep AI, but it of course also genuinely serves to try and increase the safety and proper undertaking of the task at hand. In other words, the state smog check inspector not only boosted trust for the car owner, but presumably the smog check will actually get done properly, even more so, now that the state inspector is there to monitor and guide. Such should be the same with the use of the AI Guardian Angel bot.

Notice that the AI Guardian Angel bot is not partaking directly hands-on in the performance of the task per se. Just as the state smog check inspector said that he would not be doing the smog check, it was still a task being done by the smog check specialist, and not by the state smog check inspector.

For this book, I am focusing on AI Guardian Angel bots that are there to monitor and guide the Deep AI that is undertaking the task. The AI Guardian Angel bot is not actually doing the task. This is a future extension of the concept, but I consider it not within the scope of this particular book (that's a topic for my advanced book).

Take a look at Figure 7 to see what I have tried to convey about Deep AI and the trust about Deep AI.

Deep AI and the Trust Relationship

Assertion

Consumers will have greater trust in Deep AI
by having **AI Guardian Angel Bots**
that serve to monitor and guide the Deep AI
on the behalf of the consumer and their safety.

Figure 7: Eliot – Understanding how we trust and the nature of trustworthiness

---

The next chapter offers more detailed aspects about the basis for the AI Guardian Angel bots. This chapter has provided a warm-up to get the topic of "trust" onto the table, and set the stage for what the AI Guardian Angel bots are all about.

Lance B. Eliot

CHAPTER 2

AI GUARDIAN ANGEL BOTS: KEY TO AI TRUSTWORTHINESS

Lance B. Eliot

CHAPTER 2

AI GUARDIAN ANGEL BOTS: KEY TO AI TRUSTWORTHINESS

PREFACE

In this chapter, I introduce the advent of a new line of software and systems that I refer to as the AI Guardian Angel bots. There are other names given to these emerging capabilities and we will examine what they are and why they are being formulated. The concept underlying them is relatively straightforward, namely that with the gradual and widespread use of Deep AI there will be a need to keep the inherent fragility and potentially hidden errors of Machine Learning from readily producing harmful results.

How are people going to be willing to trust these Deep AI systems? One answer involves fighting fire-with-fire, so to speak, by using specialized systems or bots that will observe the Deep AI and then provide a means to gauge whether the Deep AI is diverging toward inadvertent harmful results. If an AI Guardian Angel bot detects anomalous behaviors, it will either emit recommendations to the Deep AI system in the hopes of averting the harmful results, and/or will override the Deep AI system in cases where such an override is feasible and permitted.

It is my prediction that this new line of AI Guardian Angel bots will become increasingly valued by the marketplace. Once Deep AI has been placed into circumstances wherein harmful results are highly visible, such as self-driving cars, there will be a backlash and strident calls to rein in Deep AI, and for which then the AI Guardian Angel bots will be one significant means to solve this problem, and a new market will be born.

CHAPTER 2:

AI GUARDIAN ANGEL BOTS: KEY TO AI TRUSTWORTHINESS

Deep AI is being infused into modern day systems and provides intelligent-like behavior that can greatly enhance the capabilities of other technologies and machinery. There are tremendous benefits that will accrue due to the use of AI and machine learning in everyday systems. One of the most visible such examples involves self-driving cars. As will be discussed in this chapter, the hope for self-driving cars is that the adoption of Deep AI will allow cars to be driven by automation rather than a human, and ultimately these automation-driven cars will reduce the number of fatalities and injuries on-the-road. Besides providing life-or-death improvements, self-driving cars will radically change other aspects of business and society.

Unfortunately, we must also consider the potential downside of the use of Deep AI for self-driving cars and any other machinery that has the possibility of inadvertent harmful results. I will refer to Figure 1 as a means to explain why there is a possibility of harmful results occurring when Deep AI is deployed.

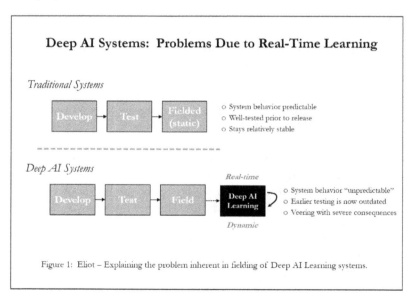

Figure 1: Eliot – Explaining the problem inherent in fielding of Deep AI Learning systems.

As an aside, I am asserting that there is a downside to Deep AI systems not because I am a Luddite that wants to stop the progress of Deep AI and its application, but instead because I am concerned on behalf of all parties that there might be a backlash against Deep AI, and perhaps rightfully so if there are not sufficient protections provided in how such systems are adopted and placed into the real-world. Plus, of course, and more importantly, I have concerns about the outcomes of the inadvertent harmful results. I firmly believe that those that create such systems should also be dutifully considering how to ensure that such systems are able to be safe and secure, and guard against inadvertent harmful results. There are also potential regulatory impacts and other legal ramifications that will arise, as we will discuss further in this chapter.

For those of you that are philosophically minded, there has long been bandied about the role of scientists and engineers when they create "Frankenstein" like advances – I am not going to weigh into that debate here, but just point the reader to that body of literature in case you are interested in learning more about it. I am going to remain more practical herein.

DEEP AI VERSUS TRADITIONAL SYSTEMS

We can likely all agree that any Deep AI system is bound to have some kinds of flaws within the system itself. The odds exist. There is no means to 100% prove the reliability of a Deep AI system. I am often asked why I am especially concerned about the Deep AI systems over traditional systems.

Take a look at Figure 1. As shown, for traditional systems, we typically test the system prior to being placed into production. A battery of tests is established to try and gauge as far reaching a test set that can be practically devised within the cost and time limits for testing a system prior to it being fielded. Some systems are well tested prior to release, while others are at times poorly tested. If the system is say a word processing application, perhaps our testing can be a bit less exhaustive. On the other hand, if the system controls a robotic arm in a manufacturing plant and for which human workers interact, we would certainly hope and anticipate that more exhaustive testing would be undertaken.

In any case, once a traditional system is placed into production or use, its behavior is relatively predictable. By this I mean that the software itself remains somewhat stable while it is in use. It is not typically self-changing itself while in use. On the other hand, Deep AI systems are by-design intended to change while in use. It is often an integral part of the reason they are made use of. Over time, their behavior is intended to "learn" by self-modification and presumably improve with time.

This is a crucial point to comprehend about Deep AI systems. The import is that we cannot particularly know at the time prior to release what the Deep AI system will do once it is released. We can test as much as we like or can, prior to production, but after it is available in use, those tests are essentially outdated. The remaining "testing" once it goes into use is pretty much what the Deep AI actually does while in the field.

There are critics that have accused Tesla of allowing their self-driving capabilities to be essentially a grand experiment of in-the-field testing by those that have purchased and drive Tesla cars. Some would say that Tesla has been "lucky" so far that they have not had any significant backlash to this approach. The fatality of Joshua Brown, a Tesla S driver that was killed in a road incident on May 7, 2016, has become the first reported fatality involving the Tesla while it was in the automated control mode. To-date, it has been reported that the automation was unable to detect a tractor-trailer that was making a left turn in front of the Tesla, supposedly undetected because the white side of the truck blended with the brightly lit sky, and presumably had the automation detected the truck it would have applied the brakes of the Tesla to try and avoid the crash.

I am using the word "presumably" in describing the incident because we, the public, have yet to gain any complete indication of the actual incident and what the Tesla car did or did not do. At this point, it is speculation and conjecture. We might assume that what we know now is a true indication. Or, it could be that perhaps the automation of the Tesla detected the truck but made the wrong "decision" about what action to take, such as not taking any action at all. Or, it could be that the Tesla detected the truck and tried to invoke the brakes, but perhaps something about the automation failed and did not engage the brakes. Etc.

Let's also make clear in this discussion about Deep AI that traditional systems are not flawless, even though they are more amenable to testing and do not tend to alter themselves while in use. Traditional systems have proven themselves time-and-again to have flaws within them, and there are thousands and thousands of examples of how conventional systems have produced harmful results, in spite of being tested prior to release. Very extensive testing and Quality Assurance (QA) efforts for traditional automation is not a guarantee of purity of results. Traditional systems and their flaws have indeed caused harmful results. Much of the time, people have been able to avoid the harmful results due to being directly involved in the actions of the conventional system. For example, in the case of cars, our use of cruise control can be relatively quickly disengaged and the human driver take over control of the car.

The point is that we already know that traditional systems can and will have flaws that can produce harmful results (in spite of being more testable), and so we might reasonably expect that Deep AI systems will have at least as many such chances for flaws and perhaps even more so due to the nature of how Deep AI systems work. When you also add into this calculus that Deep AI systems tend to use Artificial Neural Networks

(ANN), which are essentially simulations of neuron-like aspects, the ability to interpret the logical meaning of an ANN is extremely low, it has very little transparency, and so the software engineers or developers cannot even say with clarity why the ANN is working properly or improperly per se. This would be in stark contrast to conventional coding, whereby an inspection of the programming code could ascertain where the system had failed to operate or was incorrectly logically coded such that it produced an error or flawed result.

DEEP AI BACKLASH BY STAKEHOLDERS

We can therefore anticipate that once Deep AI is more widely deployed, we will gradually begin to see the emergence of harmful results by the Deep AI elements. Aspects to anticipate include that we will experience unexpected behavior, undesired behavior, deadly behavior, wild behavior, costly behavior, illegal behavior, immoral behavior, and so on. Take a look at Figure 2.

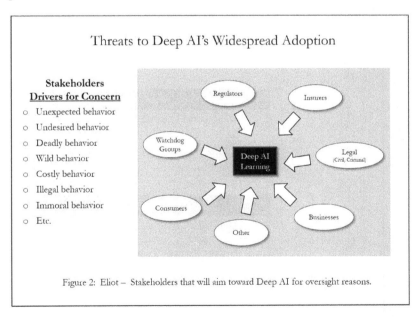

Figure 2: Eliot – Stakeholders that will aim toward Deep AI for oversight reasons.

Once the initial unbridled excitement about Deep AI begins to wane and becomes more tempered, and once the adverse consequences begin to rise in frequency and magnitude, we can easily predict that there will be a wide variety of stakeholders that will opt to heavily move in. Regulators are going to want to protect the public and show to their constituencies that they are doing something to deal with the emerging Deep AI inadvertent harmful results. Insurers are certainly going to be involved. Lawyers will jump into this pool. There are bound to be civil cases, along with the potential for criminal cases, brought against those that devised and fielded the Deep AI.

Many of the investors into this Deep AI are potentially going to find themselves shifting from being a wise investor having gotten in on the ground floor of these breathtakingly advanced systems, and instead at times find themselves trying to defend themselves and the companies that have rushed to put in place Deep AI as having been unwise investors that were apparently untroubled by the harmful results that they knew or should have known could be produced. It is going to be a mess all around.

I began the chapter by in the preface asking the question as to how will people be willing to trust these Deep AI systems? I show in Figure 3 that one approach might be to enforce that the human must be involved in the Deep AI system such that the human can co-control whatever machinery is involved, such as a self-driving car that allows for the human to take over the controls when needed. There are many problems involved in allowing the person to become engaged in co-control.

Deep AI Systems: Problems in Ensuring Trust

Humans Can't Do It	Human Control of Deep AI Real-Time Systems	
	i	Cognitive dissonance problem
	ii	Reaction time problem
	iii	Controls access problem
	iv	False reaction problem

Conventional Testing Can't Do It	Testing of Deep AI Real-Time Systems	
	i	Developer overload in testing scope
	ii	Constrained non-real-world testing limitations
	iii	Real-world open testing as lagging and off-target
	iv	Built-in test capabilities are suspect and biased

Figure 3: Eliot – Aspects of inherent limitations in overseeing Deep AI in real-time.

WHY HUMANS CAN'T DO IT

As listed in Figure 3, the cognitive dissonance problem is that there can be a gap cognitively between what the automation "knows" and what the person knows, and so at the time of hand-off between automation to human that the human is unaware of what is taking place and what action they are supposed to undertake. I've covered this topic in my book entitled "On Being a Smart CIO" in the chapter on Human-Computer Interaction (HCI), so I won't repeat those aspects here.

Suffice it to say here that this cognitive dissonance can mean that the human, even when handed control, would be unable or unaware of what action must be taken to mitigate or avoid the impending harmful result. In the case of the Tesla incident with Joshua Brown, suppose that the automation had suddenly handed control to him, would he have even realized that the reason the hand-off occurred was because of the truck making the left turn, or it could be for many other potential reasons that he otherwise would not have known about or mentally tried to conjure.

Another aspect of why co-control is problematic includes the reaction time problem. The human might not have time to react once co-control is offered or taken. Again, the Tesla incident is handy to speculate about, suppose that the automation did hand the control over to the driver, and suppose he even realized the truck was turning in front of him, would he have had sufficient time to apply the brakes to avoid or reduce the crash? Possibly not.

Finally, we can also consider that handing control over to the human might involve the controls access problem, whereby the person might not be able to readily access the controls. Imagine if a self-driving car switches the driving over to the driver, but the driver has their hands holding a burger and soda, and the feet and legs of the human driver are not near to the floor pedals. There is also the false reaction problem, whereby the automation hands control over to the human, they think that an imminent accident is about to occur and so react by slamming on their brakes, but suppose it would have been better to accelerate rather than brake, and so the human causes a worse consequence by undertaking a false reaction

CONVENTIONAL TESTING CAN'T DO IT

Figure 3 also indicates the reasons why conventional testing is not going to ensure that Deep AI does not produce potentially harmful results. Beyond my earlier point about Deep AI being self-altering while in use, and its lack of transparency or opaqueness, we can also toss into this the developer bias of what they think needs to be tested, the lack of ability to test under real-world conditions prior to release, and so on.

INFLECTION POINT FOR TRUST OF DEEP AI

So far in this chapter, I have tried to make the business case that there is an impending point at which the advent of Deep AI in widespread use will bring forth the realization and concern about these systems producing inadvertent harmful results, and that once this emerges there will be a bandwagon of stakeholders that will jump onto the topic.

I see this as inexorably moving toward an inflection point, as shown in Figure 4. As you can see in Figure 4, consumer acceptance is on the vertical axis, while time is on the horizontal axis. We are in the initial stages of Deep AI deployment and there is initial enthusiasm about it. I assert that we will rise to a crest at which time there will be sufficient catastrophes that a tipping point is reached. There will then be a downward trend as the bandwagon gets underway about needing to do something about the untrustworthiness of Deep AI. We will then end-up in a trough, out of which either Deep AI will founder, or it will resurge.

It is my contention that Deep AI can resurge if there is proper adoption of AI Guardian Angels, which I shall describe next in this chapter.

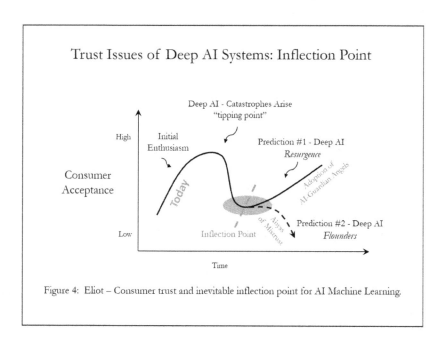

Figure 4: Eliot – Consumer trust and inevitable inflection point for AI Machine Learning.

AI GUARDIAN ANGEL BOTS

How will people come to trust Deep AI? I propose that trustworthiness will arise if the Deep AI can be prevented from producing these inadvertent harmful results, and that we can do so to some extent by fighting fire-with-fire, so to speak, and use automation to help avert potential inadvertent harmful results of Deep AI. Some are calling this a form of AI oversight, some are calling it AI guardians or overseers. There have been even some suggestions that it should be called an AI vigilante, AI caretaker, AI custodian, and so on.

For ease of naming this, I am going to call them AI Guardian Angels, and then add the word "bots" to it. In total, it is then referred to as AI Guardian Angel Bots. My rationale for this naming is that the phrasing of "Guardian Angels" has an immediate and positive connotation to it, more so than simply AI Guardian might, and I have added the word "bots" to denote that this is software that is serving as the AI Guardian Angel. I suppose some might otherwise think that the AI Guardian Angel is a human or some kind of mystical thing or creature.

In Figure 5, I show that there are three trust zones. The inner zone is Deep AI with no particular checks-and-balances at run time, which is going to undermine trust by people. There are conventional checks-and-balances at the second zone, which will help to aid trust, but the weakness of those conventional checks-and-balances will be insufficient. The third and final zone is the AI Guardian Angel bots. This would provide strong checks-and-balances and will help aid trust.

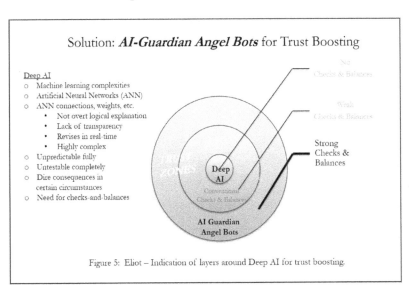

Figure 5: Eliot – Indication of layers around Deep AI for trust boosting.

When I say that the AI Guardian Angel bots will aid trust, I am not saying it will guarantee trust. It will enhance the trustworthiness of Deep AI. I am anticipating that consumers, businesses, society overall will gradually have an expectation that there are AI Guardian Angels put in place to oversee the Deep AI that they are encountering, and provide a means to try and prevent or mitigate especially dire adverse consequences.

The analogy might be to your house. My house without any kind of burglar detection capability is safe to a certain degree of trust. By adding a burglar detection capability, such as an alarm when a window is broken, I am increasing trust in the safety of my house. If I also have an armed guard patrolling my house, it is another added sense of trust. The AI Guardian Angel bots will be akin to that kind of added layer of safety that will imbue added trust into Deep AI.

FOUR STAGE ACTION MODEL

I show in Figure 6, my four stage action model depicting what the AI Guardian Angel bots will do. I explain this model next.

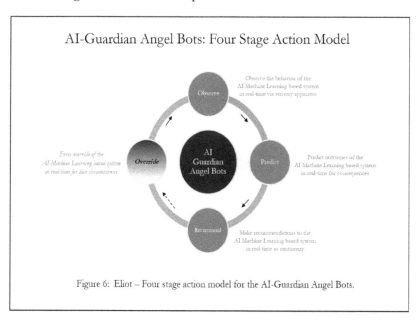

Figure 6: Eliot – Four stage action model for the AI-Guardian Angel Bots.

There are four stages to the model. Each stage has a distinct purpose. The first two stages are always occurring, while the third and fourth stages will occur only in certain circumstances. Let's explore this further.

STAGE 1: OBSERVE

The AI Guardian Angel bot is tasked to Observe the behavior of the Deep AI.

This involves obtaining sufficient sensory and other data to be able to assess the current status of whatever machinery is using the Deep AI. Notice that I am referring to observing the Deep AI, which does not necessarily mean probing into the Deep AI itself. Instead, the AI Guardian Angel bot is external to the Deep AI and not reaching per inside the internals of the Deep AI, but instead focusing on what behavior is exhibited by the Deep AI.

In the case of self-driving cars, the AI Guardian Angel bot might be tapping into the sensory data of the car, and using its own algorithms to analyze the sensory data. My analogy would be that suppose you have a human driving a conventional car, and you have a passenger in the car that is also paying attention to the road. The passenger is receiving essentially the same sensory data as the driver (not quite, but let's pretend so), and so can be simulating driving the car themselves, even though the driver is actually operating the controls.

STAGE 2: PREDICT

The second stage is the Predict stage. Here, the AI Guardian Angel bot tries to predict what might happen next, making use of the sensory data and whatever other algorithms the bot has.

Imagine again that you are a passenger in a car, you are paying attention to the road, you are also predicting what might happen next. If you see that a car ahead of you has engaged its brakes, you might likely predict that the driver of the car you are in should also be applying the brakes. You collected sensory data, analyzed it, and made a prediction.

STAGE 3: RECOMMEND

The third stage is the Recommend stage. Here, the AI Guardian Angel bot upon making a prediction will ascertain whether or not to make a recommendation to the Deep AI. Continuing my analogy, if you are human passenger and see a car ahead that was applying its brakes, you might turn to the driver of your car and suggest to them that they ought to be applying the brakes too. You would not always make such a recommendation, in that suppose you also could see that the driver of your car was already applying the brakes. In other words, the Recommend stage only occurs in circumstances for which the bot upon making a prediction has ascertained that a recommendation to the Deep AI is warranted.

STAGE 4: OVERRIDE

In the fourth stage of the model, the AI Guardian Angel bot might override the Deep AI, as based upon the other three stages of having observed, predicted, and recommended. Using again my analogy of humans in a conventional car, suppose the passenger is observing the road, sees the car ahead braking, says to the driver of the car they are in that they should consider braking too, but then suppose the driver does not opt to apply the brakes. The passenger might override the driver, and reach over to force the brakes to be applied, perhaps pushing the leg of the driver downward onto the brakes.

This override stage would typically be a last ditch effort. It would not be the norm. Presumably, in my analogy, you have overall trust for the human driver of the car you are in, and so you are more than likely to at most offer a recommendation while they are driving. It would only be in the most dire of circumstances that you might try to override and take control of the car. Imagine if the driver suddenly suffered a heart attack and you have to take over the wheel of the car. It does happen, though obviously with fortunately very low frequency. Such should be the case for the AI Guardian Angel bot.

BLUE OCEAN (NEW MARKET)

I have been using the example of cars to illustrate the nature of making use of an AI Guardian Angel bot, but you should not envision this capability in such a narrow manner. Instead, it can be seen as a capability that would be used with nearly any kind of Deep AI system.

Suppose we have a smart toaster, which has Deep AI elements to it. Exciting, you can have your toast made to your particular liking, and the Deep AI does all sorts of other fancy things to enhance your toast. Could we use an AI Guardian Angel bot for this? And if so, why would we do so (i.e., what would be the benefit to outweigh whatever cost there might be to having the bot)?

Let's suppose the Deep AI is pretty good at making toast. One day, though, the Deep AI inadvertently leaves the bread toasting for too long, and the toast begins to burn, possibly leading to a fire. The Deep AI might not realize the pending danger. An AI Guardian Angel bot that was crafted for smart toasters that have Deep AI, might save the day, which I explain next.

The toaster-aimed AI Guardian Angel bot is continually observing the toaster, doing so via the sensory aspects of the toaster (Observe stage). It is making predictions (Predict stage), such as whether the toast will come out properly or not. Suppose the bot ascertains that the toast is taking overly long to be made, and maybe even picks up from a heat sensor of the toaster that the toaster itself is reaching dangerous levels. The bot might then Recommend (Stage 3) to the smart toaster that it disengage the toast, hoping that the Deep AI will abide and do so before the toast catches on fire. If the smart toaster does not abide, and if the bot ascertains that the fire is imminent, it Overrides (Stage 4) the smart toaster per se and ejects the toast.

You might say that the human wanting the toast should have seen that the toaster was getting toward catching on fire. But, recall that with a smart toaster, the human probably is in another room, figuring no need to watch their smart toaster. Only once the flames and smoke have occurred, might the human realize they need to intervene, and it might be too late.

I refer to the AI Guardian Angel bots as a "Blue Ocean" which is a somewhat popular business term meaning that it is essentially a new market (in contrast, a so-called "Red Ocean" in a market that has many competitors and has been bloodied as they duke it out for market share). There aren't particularly such bots yet today. I see them as becoming increasingly popularized once Deep AI becomes more pervasive in the real-world. See Figure 7, showing that the AI Guardian Angel bots are on the horizon.

Figure 7: Eliot – Few can yet see the emergence of the AI-Guardian Angels bots

SELF-DRIVING CARS AND TRUST

I will continue this discussion about the AI Guardian Angel bots and revisit the topic of self-driving cars. I do so because the advent of self-driving cars is upon us, it has received incredible attention in the marketplace and society, and it offers a readymade example of the basis for having AI Guardian Angel bots. Just please remember that such bots can be applied in many other Deep AI circumstances.

The Society of Automotive Engineers (SAE) have provided a handy indication of the levels of automation possible for a car. See Figure 8. The Level 0 is no automation and the human driver is fully driving the car. Level 1 is Driver Assisted, Level 2 is Partial Automation, Level 3 is Conditional Automation, Level 4 is High Automation, and Level 5 is Full Automation. The shaded portion shows that the level of automation is rising as you get to higher levels, starting from 0 and ranging up to the maximum of 5.

I would assert that the need for Deep AI is also illustrated by the shading, in that the Deep AI is how we will get to those higher levels of automation. I would then also as a corollary assert that the need for AI Guardian Angel bots rises correspondingly too. In other words, the deeper the Deep AI, the more the need for the AI Guardian Angel bots that would be crafted specifically for these self-driving cars.

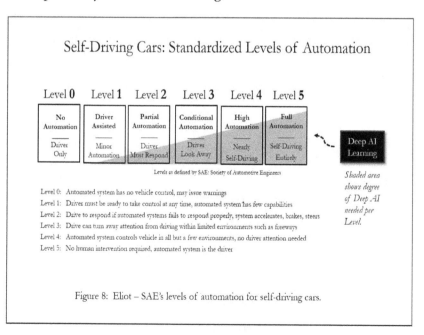

Figure 8: Eliot – SAE's levels of automation for self-driving cars.

We next turn to the topic of trust. You are a human driver sitting in a Level 3 self-driving car. Should you trust the self-driving car? Suppose you are in a Level 4, would you trust it? Suppose you are in a Level 5, would you trust it? Let's think about the nature of trust and unpack it.

Take a look at Figure 9. In what way do we as humans trust other human drivers of cars? I suggest that if you were asked about a race car professional as to how good a driver they are, your trust level might be quite high, since you perceive them as being trained in and very road-versed in terms of driving a car. The same might be said of a trained police officer, though maybe your perceive them as not quite as a good a driver as a professional race car driver. A limo driver is maybe next, and then a taxi cab driver below that.

You might have distrust for some kinds of drivers. For example, surveys show that many people have some distrust of senior citizens that are drivers. Likewise, they have distrust for teenage drivers, whom they perceive as newbies in driving and also generally reckless in behavior. Your magnitude of distrust might get quite magnified for a drunk driver, which we would assume is not in complete control of their own faculties and so therefore likely to drive erratically and dangerously. A car chase driver would presumably be even worse on this trust scale, since they are usually desperate and have no or little regard for anyone else on the road.

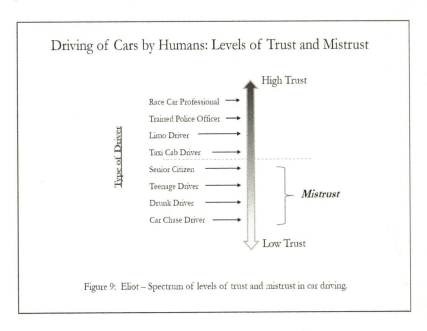

Figure 9: Eliot – Spectrum of levels of trust and mistrust in car driving.

My point is that trust of drivers is relative and not just a single monolith. We perceive trust based upon the nature of the driver. The driver and their circumstances in terms of prior driving history, reputation, and so on, are all factors in whether we are willing to trust that driver and also how much distrust we have for that driver.

Let's next then take a look at Figure 10. Here, you can see that we have placed a human driver onto our trust scale, along with the Deep AI as a driver. Consumer perception right now is that the human driver is likely more trustworthy than the Deep AI driver.

For some, such as Tesla S drivers, they might argue that they tend to believe in the self-driving car automation more so than many human drivers. And, of course, we can get there by comparing the automation to say a drunk driver, which probably most might be willing to agree the automation might be safer than.

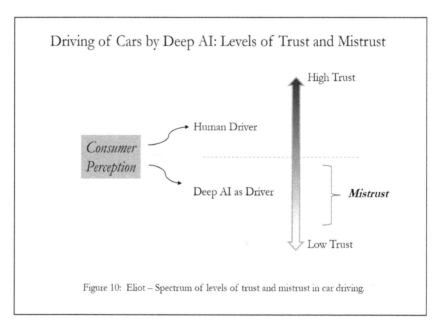

Figure 10: Eliot – Spectrum of levels of trust and mistrust in car driving.

This gives attention to one important aspect about the trust of self-driving cars. As they say, beauty is in the eye of the beholder. I mean to say that depending upon your personal viewpoint and contact with self-driving cars, your opinion of their trustworthiness will vary. Some exhibit great faith in self-driving cars, while others are adamantly mistrustful of self-driving cars.

A recent Kelly Blue Book survey found that more than half of those surveyed would prefer to retain full control of their cars, and this was when pressed that it could means that roads might be less safe than if all cars were self-driving cars.

Similar to other innovations and their adoption, we can apply a classic technology adoption curve to the consumer trust levels of self-driving cars. Take a look at Figure 11. Tesla S drivers are likely in the leftmost bracket of "innovators" that are a very small percentage of total drivers, and thus we must be mindful that when they faithfully offer their belief in self-driving cars it represents only a tiny segment of the driving population.

Indeed, in spite of the Joshua Brown crash, Tesla S drivers appear to be as ever faithful to their cars as they were before the incident (surveys seem to suggest this). These are true believers, and it will take a lot more than one crash, and a crash that still is vaguely understood, in order to shake them from their faith. Had the crash more overtly revealed unambiguously flaws in the automation, it might have done more to undermine these true believers.

Self-driving cars have not yet even reached the Early Adopters, let alone the Early Majority. And then trying to get the Late Majority on-board and finally the Laggards, well, it will be a long bumpy road ahead for adoption, as they say.

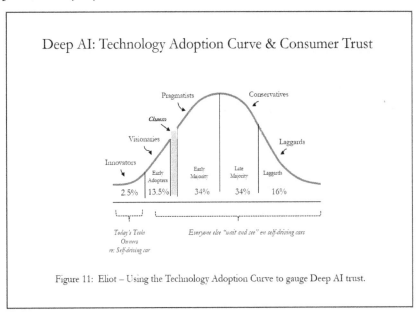

Figure 11: Eliot – Using the Technology Adoption Curve to gauge Deep AI trust.

It is relatively predictable to anticipate that once the Early Adopters jump in, and then if we have more incidents like Joshua Brown, the stakeholders that I mentioned earlier will be more likely to get engaged. The Early Adopters are not likely going to be as forgiving as the Innovators.

AI GUARDIAN ANGEL BOTS & CARS

Let's then get back to the notion of trust levels. Take a look at Figure 12. As shown, we have augmented the earlier chart shown in Figure 10. Now, we have unpacked so-to-speak the truly self-driving car by saying that we have two such circumstances. We have the "Deep AI with Oversee Driver" which is the method being used these days by some of the self-driving car developing companies. They have a human driver in the car to ensure that if it goes a kilter the human driver will takeover (Uber and Google has been using this practice for now).

Then there are those that are trying the "Deep AI Solo as Driver" approach. For now, the trust by consumers of self-driving cars is generally that with the Oversee Driver they have more trust than when the self-driving car has no such Oversee Driver. I have placed the "Deep AI with Oversee Driver" above even the human driver level of trust, which I do because some might view the combination of automation and human driver as being even safer than a human driver alone. This can of course be easily argued, but anyway, we'll go with this for the moment.

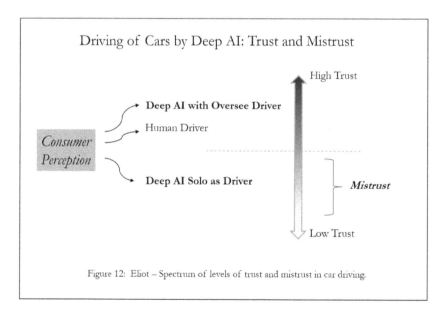

Figure 12: Eliot – Spectrum of levels of trust and mistrust in car driving.

I am taking you toward thinking about where the self-driving car that would have an AI Guardian Angel bot might then fit on this trust scale. Let's take a look.

As shown in Figure 13, I have placed the Deep AI that is augmented with an AI-Guardian Angel bot as somewhere between the Deep AI with Oversee Driver and the Human Driver.

The basis for this placement is that assuming that the AI Guardian Angel bot is well-built and provides the oversight expected, it would presumably be better than the Oversee Driver since it can react in a manner that avoids our earlier concerns about why humans can't do so (refer again to Figure 3).

But, this belief in the AI Guardian Angel bot will only be the case if such bots are well designed and shown to do what they are intended to do. If such bots are brought into the marketplace and they themselves are weak and flawed, it would naturally undermine the belief that they add any substantive second layer of safety. In fact, if such a bot were to override an existing Deep AI system and it turned out that the override was the wrong action, it certainly could dampen the market and growth of such bots.

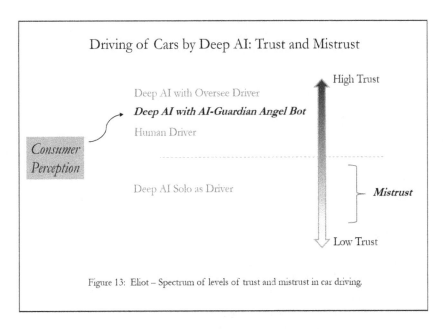

Figure 13: Eliot – Spectrum of levels of trust and mistrust in car driving.

Surveys of consumers show that they have less faith in the car manufacturers to make self-driving cars than they do in high-tech firms to be able to do so. This is partially due to the glow of the high-tech firms as to being at the cutting edge of technology. Car manufacturers tend to be perceived as being behind on technology and not the best choice therefore for making a technology-based car, in comparison to high-tech firms.

Car manufacturers have had important moments of public distrust. As shown in Figure 14, the Ford Edsel became famous as a car that was overhyped, unattractive, and overpriced. This created a sense of image distrust for car manufacturers. To this day, we even use the word Edsel as a derogatory term when referring to any product that is a dud or potential dud.

An even worse occurrence of distrust arose during the famous Ford Pinto episode. As depicted on Figure 14, the Ford Pinto had rear fuel tank placement issues that led to low-speed rear-end crashes producing fiery results. This led to lawsuits and even criminal prosecution for the car manufacturer and other allied businesses associated with the Ford Pinto.

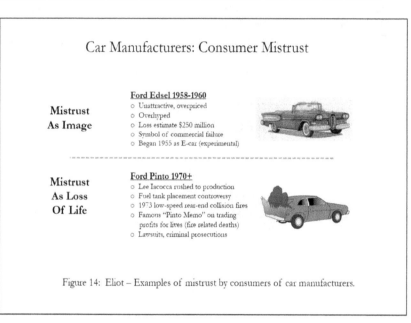

Figure 14: Eliot – Examples of mistrust by consumers of car manufacturers.

This begs the question as to whether the advent of self-driving cars might be headed in the same direction. Though the world looks rosy right now and there are many clamoring for the self-driving cars, we can anticipate that self-driving cars are not going to be perfect out-the-gate (if ever). The nature of the imperfections and the expectations and promises to consumers will all come to play.

I offer these thoughts not so much as an aspect about the AI Guardian Angel bots, but also to forewarn about what self-driving cars can and cannot do, and what the limits are of Deep AI towards providing self-driving cars. And too, the potential importance of applying AI Guardian Angel bots to the mix.

SYSTEMS: AI GUARDIAN ANGEL BOTS

Let's get back to the AI Guardian Angel bots, which as a reminder are not tied to self-driving cars and that I was only using self-driving cars as an illustrative example. These oversight bots can be used for pretty much any circumstance, not only for Deep AI oversight, which is where they are most needed perhaps, but even can be used in circumstances where there is no or little AI involved in the underlying system being overseen.

For the moment, we'll focus on their role related to Deep AI systems. Take a look at Figure 15. We have a Deep AI system that has some form of internal memory and some kind of access to sensory devices in real-time. This is our smart toaster, our smart self-driving car, etc. There will be AI Guardian Angel bots that are aimed at particular machinery, such as a family of such bots for self-driving cars. We might anticipate such a AI Guardian Angel bot for Ford cars, for BMW cars, and so on. One might also anticipate that such bots will be needed for the Internet of Things, such as the household smart refrigerator, washer, dryer, etc.

We will be covering more of the facets shown in Figure 15 in the next chapter. For now, one of the most significant aspects will be the use of API's into the Deep AI systems, along with the nature of the coordination and collaboration between the AI Guardian Angel bots and the Deep AI systems. For example, how to provide a Recommendation to the Deep AI system and its response, along with how an Override would occur. Those details are covered in the next chapter.

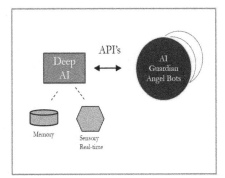

AI-Guardian Angel Bots: Systems Aspects

- Families of AI-Guardian Bots
- By Products, IoT
- API's to Deep AI systems
- Ratings of AI-Guardian Bots
- Certified Deep AI re: AI-G Bots
- Override Agreed Protocols
- Recommender Agreed Protocols
- Sensory Apparatus Access
- Security & System Co-Trust
- Manufacturers Selection & Adoption
- Consumer Selection & Adoption

Figure 15: Eliot – Systems aspects for next steps in emergence of AI-Guardian Angel Bots

I would predict that there will be a slew of these AI Guardian Angel bots, offered by third-party developers to major high-tech firms. These specialized bots will at times be independently developed, independent of the underlying system that they are overseeing. For example, company X might develop a bot for the Tesla self-driving car that consumers might purchase separately and apart from Tesla. In other cases, the original manufacturer or maker might provide the AI Guardian Angel bot, packaged with the rest of the core system itself.

PARRALEL MARKET TO DEEP AI MARKET

As shown in Figure 16, the Deep AI systems market of AI and Machine Learning is growing rapidly.

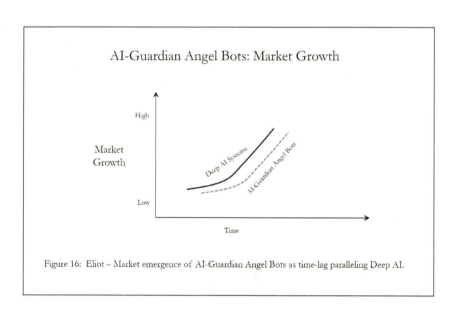

Figure 16: Eliot – Market emergence of AI-Guardian Angel Bots as time-lag paralleling Deep AI.

I predict that the AI Guardian Angel bots market will grow similarly, though on a slight time lag delay. The basis for the time lag delay is that until the market realizes that inherent possibility of the Deep AI systems producing inadvertent harmful results, there will not likely be much of a clamor for the bots. Once the bots are introduced and if they perform as intended, there will be a wave of demand that such bots be provided to the market.

We will continue our exploration of the systems nature of the AI Guardian Angel bots in the next chapter. This chapter has provided an introduction to the topic and made a business case for the advent of these new systems, laying appropriate groundwork for getting into further detail.

CHAPTER 3

API'S FOR DEEP AI AND AI GUARDIAN ANGEL BOTS

CHAPTER 3

API'S FOR DEEP AI AND AI GUARDIAN ANGEL BOTS

PREFACE

One of the popular and important trends in the high-tech field is the advent of Application Programming Interfaces (API's). Though API's have been around for a long time, we have seen more recently an expanded view of the value in API's. Essentially, they provide a kind of portal into which you can gain access to an application or possibly even a suite of applications, and presumably then utilize some kind of service or capability of that application or suite. This allows then other applications and systems to potentially make use of whatever capabilities the API-enabled application is willing to provide.

If you are writing an application for say doing reporting of a company's income and expenses, you could potentially make use of an API to have your application get such data from an accounting system that the company is using. Your application might ask for data and get it returned from the accounting system, or your application might ask the accounting application to undertake the processing for you. It all depends on what the accounting application has opted to provide via their API. Our interest in API's here is that we want to have a means to enable a Deep AI system and an AI Guardian Angel Bot to be able to communicate with each other. We will define some API's for that purpose.

———

CHAPTER 3: API'S FOR DEEP AI AND AI GUARDIAN ANGEL BOTS

API's are a hot high-tech topic these days. An Application Programming Interface (API) is simply a kind of portal that an application makes available to others for purposes of accessing the application. Though API's have been around for a long time, they have become especially valuable more recently. The rise in the number of applications available for use, along with the advent of having open source applications, provides an impetus toward wanting to readily share capabilities of one application to another application.

In our case, we are interested in API's that would allow a Deep AI system to communicate with an AI Guardian Angel bot. We need a means to be able to have the AI Guardian Angel bot make requests of the Deep AI system, and have the Deep AI system provide some kind of response. This communication is essential to the two collaborating with each other. Without the API's, the two would either not communicate, which defeats a fundamental intended purpose of the AI Guardian Angel bot, or they would need to find some other means to communicate.

For these API's, I take a logical rather than physical view of what the API's are to do and how they are undertaken. By this I mean that rather than showing a detailed specification that provides the actual parameters and such, I am providing more of a framework in this chapter. These are proposed API's and will evolve and become more substantive once the AI Guardian Angel bot catches on.

I am developing prototypes of these API's and anticipate that others in the AI community are likely doing the same.

Ultimately, there will probably need to be some kind of open source association or community around which these API's are standardized. Sometimes, a particular software maker will indicate API's that are specific to their application, but if all software makers have their own idiosyncratic API's, it becomes difficult to readily make use of those applications. If possible, it is better overall to have a public oriented API standard set, of which, specific applications would then hopefully adopt. They would be encouraged to adopt the API's as a prudent means to get their application presumably more widely accepted in the marketplace.

The indication in this chapter consists of what I consider the fundamental API's, sometimes also called the primitives. I am sure that there will be more API's that will be identified along the way of evolving the AI Guardian Angel bots ecosystem and these indicated API's will also be enhanced and improved over time.

API 1.1.0 OBSERVATION

This first API is focused on Observations. You might recall that I earlier proposed a four-stage model for the AI Guardian Angel bot, consisting of Observation, Prediction, Recommendation, and Override. I indicated that not all four stages are necessarily used all of the time. An AI Guardian Angel bot might seek observations, make predictions, and ascertain it has no need to make a recommendation and nor invoke an override.

Generally, the AI Guardian Angel bot will mainly be seeking observations and making predictions. This will be a continuous loop when the AI Guardian Angel bot has gotten underway for whatever matter is at hand. When a prediction suggests the need for a recommendation, then the AI Guardian Angel bot would enter into the third stage of producing a recommendation. If a prediction spurs the AI Guardian Angel bot to also attempt an override, then it would enter into the four stage of an override.

Each of the API's will be numbered for ease of reference. The numbering scheme is currently three numeric digits separated by periods. This first set of API's begins with the number 1. As shown in Figure 1, we have an API 1.1.0 labeled as Observation, which has the AI Guardian Angel bot emit a request (labeled as 1.1.1) to the Deep AI system for obtaining an observation. The Deep AI system then is a responder that provides it response back to the AI Guardian Angel bot (labeled as 1.1.2).

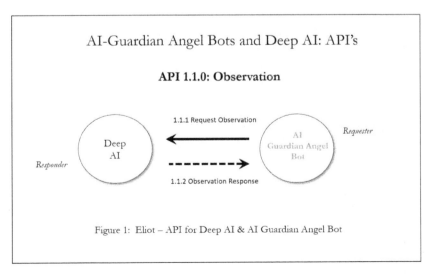

Figure 1: Eliot – API for Deep AI & AI Guardian Angel Bot

API 1.2.0 PREDICTION

Our next API is labeled as 1.2.0, as shown in Figure 2. We have bumped up the count in the digit in the middle of our labeling convention. This API is about predictions. The AI Guardian Angel bot emits a prediction that it wishes to share with the Deep AI system, doing so as a labeled in our convention as 1.2.1 to the Deep AI system. The Deep AI system then responds with some prediction response, labeled as 1.1.2.

Notice that I have not indicated in these API's the details of what is going back-and-forth between the two agents or objects (I'll occasionally refer to the Deep AI as an agent or object, and the AI Guardian Angel bot as an agent or object, which is popular parlance in the systems community). As I said earlier, this is an overall framework and the details are being evolved.

For the API 1.1.0 on Observations, the kind of observation information that might be provided to the AI Guardian Angel bot could be aspects such as if a self-driving car perhaps the current speed of the car, its direction, and other facets that are being collected by the sensors of the self-driving car. The notion is that the data would allow the AI Guardian Angel bot to analyze the status of the underlying machinery and be able to make a valid prediction of what might happen next. We will in a later chapter walk through some examples to illustrate this facet.

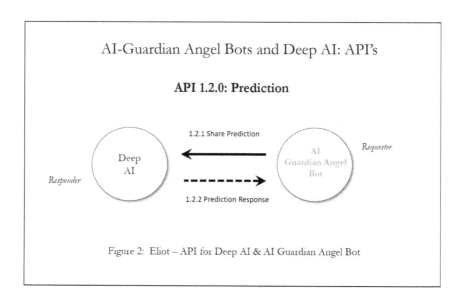

AI-Guardian Angel Bots and Deep AI: API's

API 1.2.0: Prediction

1.2.1 Share Prediction

Deep AI

AI Guardian Angel Bot

Requester

Responder

1.2.2 Prediction Response

Figure 2: Eliot – API for Deep AI & AI Guardian Angel Bot

API 1.3.0 RECOMMENDATION

We turn next to the API 1.3.0, shown in Figure 3. In this case, the AI Guardian Angel bot is share a recommendation to the Deep AI system, as labeled here as 1.3.1. The Deep AI system then might respond with a recommendation response, labeled here as 1.3.2 in our convention. Let's take a moment to consider the responses aspects coming from Deep AI to the requester AI Guardian Angel bot.

The Deep AI might provide a very helpful and definitive reply, such as in this case maybe the Deep AI might indicate that yes, it agrees with the recommendation and will enact it. Or, maybe the Deep AI will reply that it disagrees with the recommendation and has no intention of enacting it. Whatever the Deep AI replies, the AI Guardian Angel bot would consider the reply and determine what it should do next.

In some instances, perhaps upon receiving a reply that the Deep AI is going to abide by the recommendation, such as say slow down the car for a self-driving car, the AI Guardian Angel bot is satisfied for the moment that its recommendation was presumably understood and used. Of course, the AI Guardian Angel bot might continue to make observation requests, trying to ascertain whether the Deep AI is really going to carry out the recommendation or not. This is a kind of "trust but verify" notion (you might recall that famous Reagan line!).

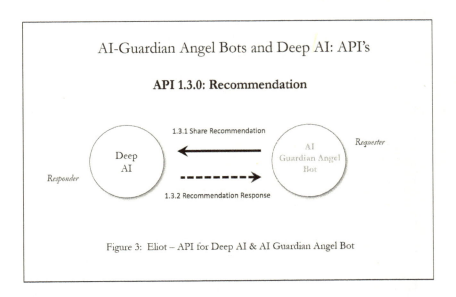

Figure 3: Eliot – API for Deep AI & AI Guardian Angel Bot

API 1.4.0 OVERRIDE

Now we are at the API 1.4.0 which has to do with overrides. See Figure 4. The AI Guardian Angel bot shares an override indicator with the Deep AI system, which we are labeling as 1.4.1 in our convention. The Deep AI systems is intended to provide a response labeled here as 1.4.2. Let's explore this API more closely.

The AI Guardian Angel bot has presumably detected something that the Deep AI is doing or not doing, and for which the result is predicted to be a harmful outcome. The AI Guardian Angel bot would likely have already shared a prediction of this outcome (via 1.2.1), and would have likely already made a recommendation of what to do about it to possibly avoid or mitigate the adverse outcome (via 1.3.1). In such a scenario, the AI Guardian Angel bot might have been informed by the Deep AI via 1.3.2 that it does not intend to undertake the recommendation. The AI Guardian Angel bot might believe this unwillingness to abide by the recommendation is so serious a mistake by the Deep AI that the AI Guardian Angel bot attempts an override. The override might be to try and force the Deep AI to accelerate the car to avoid a predicted collision.

The override is the most controversial perhaps of all of the efforts of the AI Guardian Angel bot. Should it be able to exert control over the Deep AI and force it to comply? Should it merely make a request to ask it to comply? We will be exploring in more depth these considerations later on.

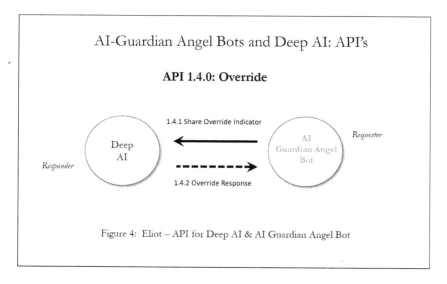

Figure 4: Eliot – API for Deep AI & AI Guardian Angel Bot

API 1.5.0 CONNECTION

In API 1.5.0, we are now doing some important housekeeping. The prior listed API's of 1.1.0, 1.2.0, 1.3.0, 1.4.0, all assumed that there was some kind of already existing connection between the Deep AI and the AI Guardian Angel bot. We actually will need to ensure explicitly that such a connection exists.

As shown in Figure 5, the AI Guardian Angel bot makes a request to the Deep AI to establish a connection, labeled here as 1.5.1. The Deep AI then provides a connection response, labeled as 1.5.2. There is more to this than perhaps meets the eye.

One aspect that will be very important about the world of Deep AI and the AI Guardian Angel bots will be to ensure that proper authentication occurs. The Deep AI is not going to want to connect with an AI Guardian Angel bot that is not trustworthy. Imagine that a stranger walks up to you and suddenly wants to carry on a dialogue with you. Why should you do so? Furthermore, suppose the stranger is an axe murderer and their intentions are evil. Don't think you want to carry on a dialogue with them. We will explore this authentication topic in more detail when we look at the ecosystem of AI Guardian Angel bots.

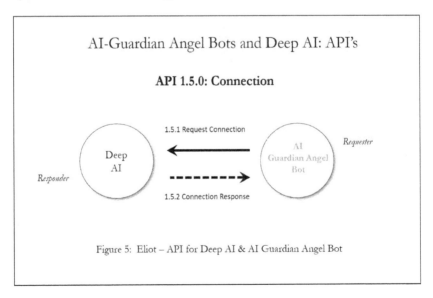

AI-Guardian Angel Bots and Deep AI: API's

API 1.5.0: Connection

1.5.1 Request Connection

Deep AI — Responder

AI Guardian Angel Bot — Requester

1.5.2 Connection Response

Figure 5: Eliot – API for Deep AI & AI Guardian Angel Bot

API 1.6.0 STATUS CHECK

We have another handy housekeeping API. This one is shown in Figure 6. The API 1.6.0 has to do with a status check. The other API's of 1.1.0, 1.2.0, 1.3.0, 1.4.0 had to do with specific stages of the model. The API 1.5.0 had to do with establishing a connection. Now, we need something to help do a status check.

It is helpful to have a means to do a status check between the Deep AI and the AI Guardian Angel bot. This might have nothing to do at all with observations, predictions, recommendations, or overrides, and be more about the AI Guardian Angel bot checking to see what's up with the Deep AI system.

For example, suppose the AI Guardian Angel bot made an observation request, our 1.1.1. After waiting a while, suppose that there is no response from the Deep AI. The AI Guardian Angel bot is getting concerned about the Deep AI. Has it fallen asleep? It is no longer connected? Is it doing something else and ignoring the AI Guardian Angel bot? The reasons for the non-response could be just about anything, and so we need to have a means to have the AI Guardian Angel bot "ping" the Deep AI and see what is taking place.

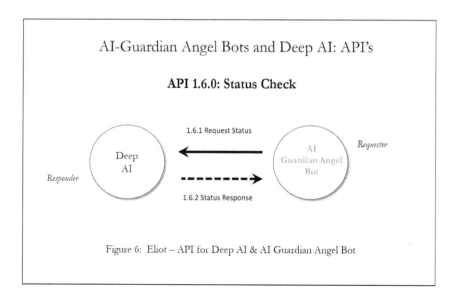

Figure 6: Eliot – API for Deep AI & AI Guardian Angel Bot

API 1.7.0 DISCONNECT

We had an API to establish a connection between the AI Guardian Angel bot and the Deep AI, which is our 1.5.0 API. Now, we need an API to make a disconnect between the AI Guardian Angel bot and the Deep AI. See Figure 7.

API 1.7.0 provides a request by the AI Guardian Angel bot to disconnect from the Deep AI, labeled as 1.7.1. The disconnect response by the Deep AI is indicated as 1.7.2. Let's explore this more closely.

First, you might think that there is no need to formally have the AI Guardian Angel bot try to disconnect. Why not just have it disconnect straight away? Well, imagine the Deep AI and it perhaps has grown fond of the AI Guardian Angel bot that is connected to it. Perhaps the AI Guardian Angel bot has been very helpful to the Deep AI in whatever task is taking place. The Deep AI might assume that the AI Guardian Angel bot is out there and covering its back, so to speak. But, if the AI Guardian Angel bot just opts to disappear and not tell anyone, the Deep AI might be caught in a lurch.

That being said, the Deep AI should already be well prepared for the inadvertent loss of the AI Guardian Angel bot, since there might be a myriad of reasons why the AI Guardian Angel bot has suddenly become disconnected. Anyway, for various sound reasons, it is handy to have a formal handshake on severing the connection.

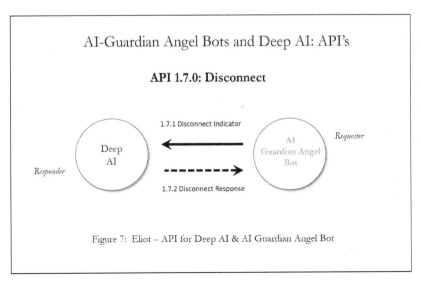

Figure 7: Eliot – API for Deep AI & AI Guardian Angel Bot

API 2.1.0 OBSERVATION

So far, the API's have all been primarily from the perspective of the AI Guardian Angel bot as the "aggressor" in that it is the agent that seeks to establish a connection, request an observation, share a recommendation, share a prediction, potentially do an override, spur a status check, and initiate a disconnect.

What about the Deep AI? Can't it also be the "aggressor" and seek to get these same actions underway? Yes, it can. You might at first be puzzled since you might be assuming that it would always and only be that the AI Guardian Angel bot is the one that steps up to the plate. And, you are right, it will usually be that way. The AI Guardian Angel bot will most of the time be the one that comes to the Deep AI and get things going.

Ultimately, you should conceive of the relationship as going both ways, being mutually reciprocal of each other. We will later on explore for example a circumstance wherein a Deep AI robot cleaner has entered into a room that it does not already know. It might seek out a proper AI Guardian Angel bot that it believes is trustworthy to help it out. Thus, we need all of the same capabilities that we had in the first set of API's, but with the direction of the requests and responses reversed.

This is the 2.x.x series of API's. Below, Figure 8 shows the first such Deep AI initiated effort, asking the AI Guardian Angel bot for an observation via 2.1.1, and the AI Guardian Angel bot responds as 2.1.2.

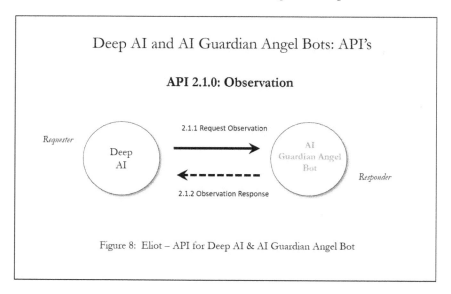

Figure 8: Eliot – API for Deep AI & AI Guardian Angel Bot

API 2.2.0 PREDICTION

In Figure 9, we have the Deep AI sharing a prediction with the AI Guardian Angel bot, labeled as 2.2.1. The AI Guardian Angel bot provides a response, labeled as 2.2.2.

Let's consider some added aspects about these API's. When a request is made, such as the 2.2.1 to share a prediction, are we guaranteed that the respondent, in this case the AI Guardian Angel bot, will actually respond? It should, and according to the API the notion is that we want to have any request be accompanied by a response. But, it is not guaranteed.

For example, suppose the AI Guardian Angel bot never actually received the 2.2.1 and so it does not know a response is being awaited by the Deep AI? Or, suppose the AI Guardian Angel bot has become disconnected from the Deep AI? There are a myriad of reasons that a response might not be forthcoming. We have the status check API's to help deal with that aspect.

We also envision that even if the respondent does not care about whatever the requester indicated, the respondent will nonetheless provide some kind of response. Suppose the requestor provides a prediction and the responder realizes it already knew that prediction. It could ignore the provided prediction and just go along on its merry way. It would be better, and certainly more polite, for it to inform the requester that the prediction was already known (and maybe have something else to indicate too).

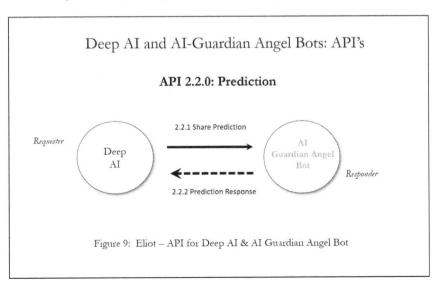

Deep AI and AI-Guardian Angel Bots: API's

API 2.2.0: Prediction

Requester — Deep AI

2.2.1 Share Prediction

2.2.2 Prediction Response

AI Guardian Angel Bot — Responder

Figure 9: Eliot – API for Deep AI & AI Guardian Angel Bot

API 2.3.0 RECOMMENDATION

In Figure 10, we have the API 2.3.0 that consists of the Deep AI sharing a recommendation to the AI Guardian Angel bot, labeled as 2.3.1. The response from the AI Guardian Angel bot is shown as 2.3.2.

Let's consider some further aspects about the nature of recommendations. In the API 1.3.0, we had the AI Guardian Angel bot share recommendations with the Deep AI. Here, we have the Deep AI share recommendations with the AI Guardian Angel bot. We will for the moment consider this as equivalent in that we don't care for the sake of discussion for the moment as to whom shared the recommendation, and we are instead interested in what the recommendation aspects are.

A recommendation is a recommendation. There, I think that defines it pretty well. Avoiding getting stuck in a recursive definition, what I mean to say is that the recommendation is not an enforceable action upon the receiver of the recommendation. If we want to enforce something such as recommendation, we would use the Override API's instead.

The notion of the recommendation is that the agent receiving it can mull it over. Maybe the recommendation provides something really nifty that the receiving agent had not previously considered. It might be a more efficient way to navigate a terrain, for example. The agent receiving the recommendation can give the recommendation due consideration, or might opt to give it short shrift. This is up to the receiving agent to ascertain.

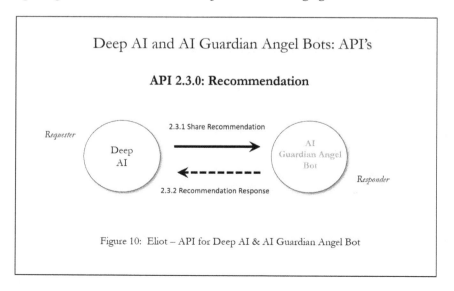

Figure 10: Eliot – API for Deep AI & AI Guardian Angel Bot

API 2.4.0 OVERRIDE

In 1.4.0, we introduced the override API. In that case, it was for the AI Guardian Angel bot that is trying to override something that the Deep AI is doing or about to do. We now have the counterpart, the Deep AI sharing an override indicator with the AI Guardian Angel bot, shown in Figure 11 and labeled as 2.4.0.

This is the one API of the 2.x.x series that is a bit different than the rest. The odds that the AI Guardian Angel bot is doing something or about to do something that the Deep AI wants to override is not normally part of the notion of the relationship between the two agents. Presumably, the AI Guardian Angel bot is usually an adviser and not partaking itself directly in some kind of machinery of acting in a manner that the Deep AI is doing.

But, for completeness, we do need to consider this as a viable possibility. For example, suppose the AI Guardian Angel bot is not only an adviser but able to control the lights in a room. Perhaps the Deep AI is trying to navigate the room, and it needs the lights on in order for its sensors to properly navigate in the room. Suppose further that the AI Guardian Angel bot has indicated to the Deep AI that the AI Guardian Angel bot intends to turn off the lights. The Deep AI might have already provided a 2.3.1 recommendation to not do so. But, perhaps it believes that the AI Guardian Angel bot is going to proceed anyway, and so now it invokes the override to prevent the lights from being turned off.

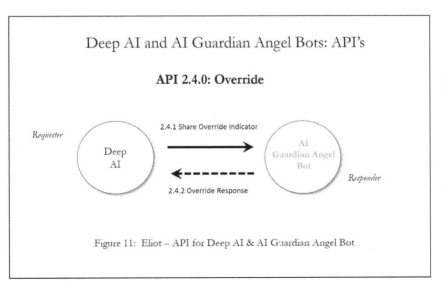

Figure 11: Eliot – API for Deep AI & AI Guardian Angel Bot

API 2.5.0 CONNECTION

In Figure 12, we provide the API 2.5.0, which is a means of trying to establish a connection. Similar to its counterpart 1.5.0, this is a request by the Deep AI to the AI Guardian Angel bot to make a connection, labeled as 2.5.1. The response by the AI Guardian Angel bot comes back to the Deep AI, via the 2.5.2.

I won't repeat the points made when discussing API 1.5.0 about why we need this API. In short, it is needed to ensure that the two agents are connecting with each and can carry out a dialogue. As mentioned before, the authentication is crucial to establishing the connection.

Let's discuss a bit more the authentication. As earlier suggested, we don't want to let just anyone connect with just anyone else. If we do so, it can be as a minimum a distraction to the agent that is legitimately doing something and then being connected to an inappropriate agent. For example, suppose a Deep AI robot cleaning a room receives a request to connect from an AI Guardian Angel bot that has to do with overseeing the self-driving car. There is presumably no cause for the Deep AI of robot cleaner to be in connection within a self-driving car AI Guardian Angel bot.

Even worse, of course, would be a bandit AI Guardian Angel bot that tries to purposely distract the Deep AI, or maybe even get the Deep AI to fall for something untoward like a rotten recommendation, or maybe try to do an override that would intentionally create harmful results. This is why the connection API's exist and authentication will be quite important.

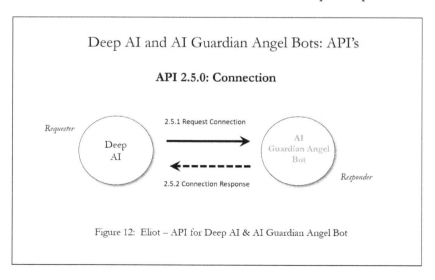

Figure 12: Eliot – API for Deep AI & AI Guardian Angel Bot

API 2.6.0 STATUS CHECK

In Figure 13, we have the API 2.6.0 which is a status check and has as its counterpart the 1.6.0 API that was earlier discussed. Here in 2.6.0, the requester is the Deep AI, requesting status via 2.6.1, and the AI Guardian Angel bot providing a status response via 2.6.2

As stated earlier for 1.6.0, we need to have a means for the two agents to share their status. In this case, the Deep AI is initiating the status request. This could be that the Deep AI has not heard from the AI Guardian Angel bot for a while, and wonders whether it is still there. Or, maybe the Deep AI made a request and has not yet gotten any reply from the AI Guardian Angel bot.

There are other kinds of status aspects, beyond just detecting presence of the other agent. Another status aspect might be to see if the AI Guardian Angel bot is brewing a prediction and if so when it might be coming over to the Deep AI. Suppose the Deep AI is navigating a room and is aware that the AI Guardian Angel bot knows the particulars of the room. The Deep AI might be in the midst of wandering around, and it assumes that the AI Guardian Angel bot will provide a prediction when warranted, but rather than waiting silently for it, the Deep AI asks about the status of it. There are many such kinds of status that might be asked about.

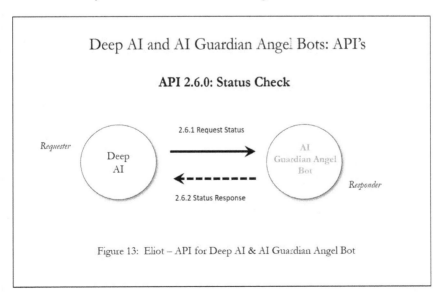

Figure 13: Eliot – API for Deep AI & AI Guardian Angel Bot

API 2.7.0 STATUS CHECK

To fully round out our API's, we'll have API 2.7.0 which is a disconnect API, and the counterpart is the 1.7.0. In this case, the Deep AI sends a disconnect indicator to the AI Guardian Angel bot, labeled as 2.7.1. The AI Guardian Angel bot provides a disconnect response, labeled as 2.7.2. As with the 1.7.0, the disconnect indication to the receiver does not necessarily mean that a disconnect will occur. This is a handshake operation whereby one party wants to disconnect, and ascertains whether the other party concurs.

We had previously noted that the receiving party might not want to disconnect. This could happen for various reasons, and mainly the notion is that the receiver wants to continue to keep the connection live. The requester can opt to disregard the response if the receiver indicates it does not want to disconnect. The receiver has already been put on notice that a disconnect might occur. Preferably, if either party wants to keep the connection open, the other party should honor it.

But, there might be good reasons that one party insists on not keeping the connection open. The collaboration aspects does not allow for somehow forcing the other party to remain connected.

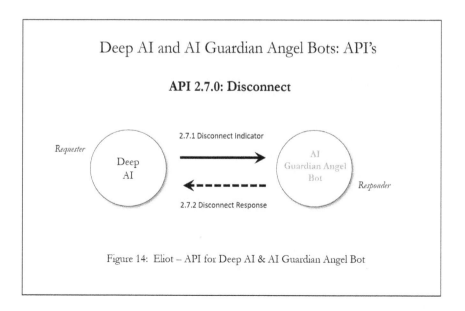

Figure 14: Eliot – API for Deep AI & AI Guardian Angel Bot

INITIATED BY AI GUARDIAN ANGEL BOT

The Figure 15 provides a handy list of the API's that are in the 1.x.x section of the API set, and consists of the API's that are originated or initiated by the AI Guardian Angel bot. For ease of reference, I have numbered them as Gnn in the leftmost column of Figure 15. There are seven API's and each has a request-to-receiver and receiver-to-requester pair, making for 14 API's.

I had indicated earlier in this chapter that these are a framework and that it is expected they will morph, be refined, expanded, etc.

Primitive API's for Deep AI & AI Guardian Angel Bot

Ref	Reference	AI Guardian Angel Bot	Deep AI	Description
G01	1.1.1	Requester	Receiver	Request Observation
G02	1.1.2	Receiver	Responder	Observation Response
G03	1.2.1	Requester	Receiver	Share Prediction
G04	1.2.2	Receiver	Responder	Prediction Response
G05	1.3.1	Requester	Receiver	Share Recommendation
G06	1.3.2	Receiver	Responder	Recommendation Response
G07	1.4.1	Requester	Receiver	Override Indicator
G08	1.4.2	Receiver	Responder	Override Response
G09	1.5.1	Requester	Receiver	Connection Request
G10	1.5.2	Receiver	Responder	Connection Response
G11	1.6.1	Requester	Receiver	Status Check
G12	1.6.2	Receiver	Responder	Status Response
G13	1.7.1	Requester	Receiver	Disconnect Indicator
G14	1.7.2	Receiver	Responder	Disconnect Response

Initiator

⬇

AI
Guardian Angel
Bot

Figure 15: Eliot – API's for Deep AI and AI Guardian Angel Bots

INITIATED BY DEEP AI

The Figure 16 provides a handy list of the API's that are in the 2.x.x section of the API set, and consists of the API's that are originated or initiated by the Deep AI. For ease of reference, I have numbered them as Dnn in the leftmost column of Figure 16. There are seven API's and each has a request-to-receiver and receiver-to-requester pair, making for 14 API's.

I had indicated earlier in this chapter that these are a framework and that it is expected they will morph, be refined, expanded, etc.

Primitive API's for Deep AI & AI Guardian Angel Bot					
Ref	**Reference**	**Deep AI**	**AI Guardian Angel Bot**	**Description**	
D01	2.1.1	Requester	Receiver	Request Observation	
D02	2.1.2	Receiver	Responder	Observation Response	
D03	2.2.1	Requester	Receiver	Share Prediction	*Initiator*
D04	2.2.2	Receiver	Responder	Prediction Response	
D05	2.3.1	Requester	Receiver	Share Recommendation	**Deep AI**
D06	2.3.2	Receiver	Responder	Recommendation Response	
D07	2.4.1	Requester	Receiver	Override Indicator	
D08	2.4.2	Receiver	Responder	Override Response	
D09	2.5.1	Requester	Receiver	Connection Request	
D10	2.5.2	Receiver	Responder	Connection Response	
D11	2.6.1	Requester	Receiver	Status Check	
D12	2.6.2	Receiver	Responder	Status Response	
D13	2.7.1	Requester	Receiver	Disconnect Indicator	
D14	2.7.2	Receiver	Responder	Disconnect Response	

Figure 16: Eliot – API's for Deep AI and AI Guardian Angel Bots

CHAPTER 4

ECOSYSTEM OF AI GUARDIAN ANGEL BOTS

CHAPTER 4

ECOSYSTEM OF
AI GUARDIAN ANGEL BOTS

PREFACE

Where are those AI Guardian Angel bots? How do you get one? You might already be aware that there are lots of ways to get "chat bots" such as for Facebook and other messenger services. Eventually, I envision a similar thriving market for the AI Guardian Angel bots. They might not have that particular naming and could be called just bots or maybe protector bots, etc., as discussed in Chapter 1 there are already various monikers given to these guardian bots.

In any case, in this chapter we'll take a look at families of AI Guardian Angel bots. There will be many ways to slice-and-dice your needs in terms of what an AI Guardian Angel bot might do for you. As will be explained, there are going to be specific circumstances where you might want to have an AI Guardian Angel bot on your side, helping you as you interact with or are at the mercy of a Deep AI system.

Not all of the uses of an AI Guardian Angel bot are for life-and-death situations. As earlier discussed, a self-driving car is indeed a potential life-or-death circumstance. Being in a self-driving car will essentially mean that you are handing over your life to automation (for cars at the higher levels of the SAE chart), and so you probably would want to have "someone" on your side to watch the self-driving automation. Imagine though other situations that aren't so dramatic and the odds are that you still might want to have an AI Guardian Angel bot on-hand. As will be discussed, something as simple as a robot cleaner in your home could benefit possibly by your using an AI Guardian Angel bot in that context.

————

CHAPTER 4: ECOSYSTEM OF
AI GUARDIAN ANGEL BOTS

AI Guardian Angel bots are so new that they are primarily in the lab or being used in pilots and prototypes. If you are familiar with Chat Bots, those kinds of bots also started out in a research and initial trial stage, and have since blossomed. Part of the reason they blossomed is due to the acceptance and promulgation of chat bots by large high-tech luminaires such as Facebook and Microsoft.

Once the AI Guardian Angel bots get past their infancy, I would anticipate that there will be an ecosystem that arises around them. I envision that there will be repositories housing AI Guardian Angel bots. Those seeking an AI Guardian Angel bot will be able to search these repositories and try to decide which ones they might want to use. Some will involve an outright fee to purchase, some will be rented, some will charge on a metered basis for use, and some will be freemium wherein there is perhaps a free low-end aspect and a charged higher end or added features version.

As mentioned earlier, the naming of these types of bots might be something other than AI Guardian Angel bots. They might be referred to as Guardian bots, Angel bots, Vigilante bots, Protector bots, and any other kind of potentially catchy or even oddball name. They might also get lumped into repositories of all other kinds of bots, such as Chat Bots. We can also assume that there will be mash-ups of Chat Bots and AI Guardian Angel bots.

The mash-up of a Chat Bot and an AI Guardian Angel bot would allow for the user of the AI Guardian Angel bot to carry on a dialogue about what they wish to have the AI Guardian Angel bot do.

If the AI Guardian Angel bot is for a self-driving car, the user of the particular AI Guardian Angel bot might indicate that they are the type of person that likes a car driving experience that is especially conservative. In which case, the AI Guardian Angel bot would keep closer tabs on the Deep AI of the self-driving car and try to ensure that the self-driving car takes a decidedly conservative driving approach.

Or, it might be that the user is desiring a bit of excitement in the driving and also late getting to work, so they want the self-driving car to take chances and go as fast as it can to get to the destination. The AI Guardian Angel bot would then presumably take such a stance related to the self-driving car. There could also be an ongoing dialogue between the AI Guardian Angel bot and the user.

For example, the user might wonder what the self-driving car is doing, and so the AI Guardian Angel bot could act to interact with the self-driving car and then interact with the user about it. Why wouldn't the user directly interact with the Deep AI of the self-driving car? They could do so, assuming that the self-driving car allows such interaction. The user though might also want to interact with the AI Guardian Angel bot, since it presumably is monitoring the self-driving car on the behalf of the user. The user might not otherwise be able to know what the self-driving car is doing. It is like having a second expert opinion, allowing the user to have an added helper in their corner.

FAMILIES OF AI GUARDIAN ANGEL BOTS

As part of the ecosystem of AI Guardian Angel bots, there could be families of various types of AI Guardian Angel bots. We will explore several such families. Let's start with a family of AI Guardian Angel bots that are focused on Deep AI that is controlling some kind of underlying machinery.

Take a look at Figure 1. Several examples of members of the family are listed.

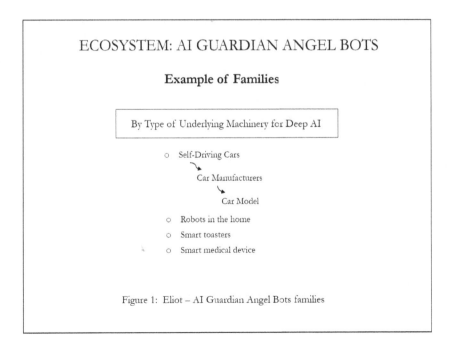

Figure 1: Eliot – AI Guardian Angel Bots families

We might have AI Guardian Angel bots that are devoted to aiding overseeing the Deep AI of self-driving cars. As such, it would be unrealistic to expect that a single AI Guardian Angel bot would be able to encompass all different kinds of self-driving cars. The odds are that AI Guardian Angel bots would be devised for specific cars of particular car manufacturers. There might be the Tesla S AI Guardian Angel bot, which would be different than the Google's self-driving cars, and so on.

So, you would look in a repository of AI Guardian Angel bots for one that is devised for your specific make and model of a self-driving car. That being said, those AI Guardian Angel bots that are for self-driving cars would have many aspects in common. They all generally would presumably be undertaking similar kinds of oversight efforts. Of course, there would be differences and the creators of the AI Guardian Angel bots would opt to provide some features in one and other features in another.

All of this is equally true for other kinds of underlying machinery that is being controlled by Deep AI. Returning to the list in Figure 1, we might have a robot in the home that you want to use an AI Guardian Angel bot for. You would look in a repository, find one that you like, and then try it out. In this case, there might be some AI Guardian Angel bots that will only work with a particular home robot system. Or, there might be AI Guardian Angel bots that will only do certain aspects of monitoring of home robot systems, such as say indoors only but not for outdoors monitoring.

Why might this be? An AI Guardian Angel bot might be developed for indoor monitoring, knowing about how to watch for robots in the kitchen, in the hallway, in the bathrooms, in the garage, in the bedrooms, and so on. But, once the robot of the home heads outside, perhaps to do something on the front porch or the back patio, the AI Guardian Angel bot might have reached its limit as to the scope of what it "knows" about. Some AI Guardian Angel bots will be very narrow in their subject matter expertise. Others will be more broadly defined.

ENVIRONMENT OF DEEP AI - FAMILY

We just covered the aspects of a family of AI Guardian Angel bots that were shaped around a Deep AI that was controlling an underlying machinery, such as a self-driving car, a home robot, a smart toaster, etc. Next, let's look at a family of AI Guardian Angel bots that is focused on particular environments. Here, the AI Guardian Angel bot might not know much about the machinery per se that the Deep AI is controlling, and instead know about the environment in which the Deep AI is trying to operate the machinery.

Take a look at Figure 2. Environments that might be considered include the home environment, the office environment, a warehouse environment, and so on.

An AI Guardian Angel bot might be an "expert" about the home environment. Thus, any machinery in the home that is being run by Deep AI could potentially come under its scope. Smart toaster, yes, the AI Guardian Angel bot can monitor it, assuming that the smart toaster has been established for connecting with AI Guardian Angel bots. Robot cleaner, yes, this too could be monitored by the AI Guardian Angel bot.

As we will see later on, one advantage of having an AI Guardian Angel bot that is focused on an environment is that the Deep AI can possibly lean upon the AI Guardian Angel bot for assistance. In other words, suppose a robot cleaner is brought into your home. Assume it has never been in your home before. How would it know where the rooms are, what chairs to avoid, what toys to not harm, etc.? The Deep AI could go on an exploration and attempt to learn these aspects of your home, which might take time to do, and might not be learned correctly. An alternative would be an AI Guardian Angel bot that knew about homes and that had become familiar already with your home specifically. It could be of help to the Deep AI of the robot cleaner (a detailed example will be explored in this book).

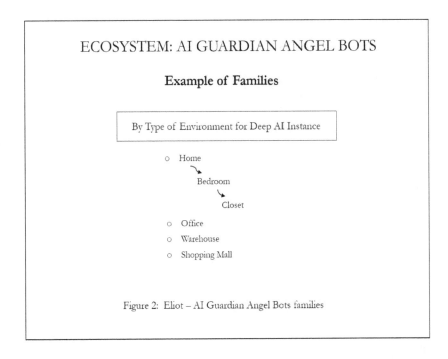

Figure 2: Eliot – AI Guardian Angel Bots families

SERVICES INVOLVING DEEP AI – FAMILY

Another type of family would be by the service involved. Take a look at Figure 3.

One type of service would be for example cleaning. Suppose the Deep AI is again a robot cleaner. You might want an AI Guardian Angel bot that is generally aware of the acts of cleaning and able to monitor any machinery that is doing cleaning. This could get specific, such as cleaning of a bathroom, and even more specific than that.

Another service would be cooking a meal. We will eventually have robotic systems that are meal preparers and cookers. There might be several robots working in concert to prepare a meal, or one that is a chef and does the preparation and cooking itself. Either way, it might be handy to have an AI Guardian Angel bot that would monitor the preparation and cooking taking place. It would be like sitting in a restaurant waiting at your table for the meal, and meanwhile having your own food inspector in the back, in the kitchen, watching over those preparing your meal.

Did they cook the meat long enough? Were they using the right ingredients that you ordered? The AI Guardian Angel bot could potentially provide oversight on those aspects.

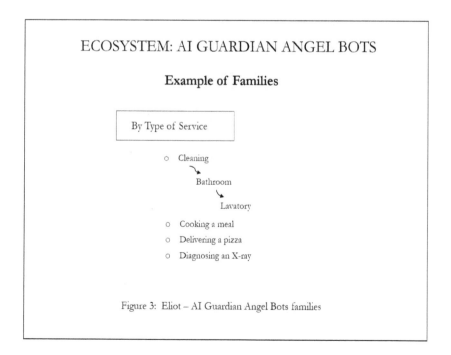

Figure 3: Eliot – AI Guardian Angel Bots families

REPOSTIRY OF AI GUARDIAN ANGEL BOTS

In recap, take a look at Figure 4. There will be repositories as part of the ecosystem of AI Guardian Angel bots. You would seek to find a desired AI Guardian Angel bot by taking a look at the repository. You might do this directly, or have someone or something (like a Chat Bot) that could do this for you.

You would likely explore the various AI Guardian Angel bots available. One way to explore them would be by the type of AI Guardian Angel bot. You might want one for your self-driving car. Another one for your home. Another one for the cooking of meals. At first, the AI Guardian Angel bots will be very narrow in scope and aimed at a particular task or Deep AI system. Over time, I would expect this to mature and expand.

You might be wondering how you would know whether an AI Guardian Angel bot is any good. Not all AI Guardian Angel bots will be equal in terms of what they do. Even ones aimed at the same aspect, let's say there are several AI Guardian Angel bots aimed at Tesla cars, you would want some form of rating to help you ascertain which is best for you. We will cover this topic of ratings of AI Guardian Angel bots in the next chapter.

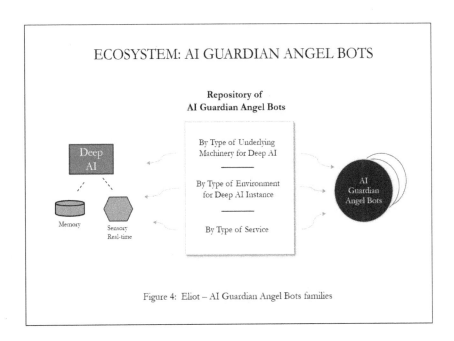

ECOSYSTEM: AI GUARDIAN ANGEL BOTS

Figure 4: Eliot – AI Guardian Angel Bots families

CHAPTER 5
RATINGS FOR
AI GUARDIAN ANGEL BOTS

Lance B. Eliot

CHAPTER 5

RATINGS FOR
AI GUARDIAN ANGEL BOTS

PREFACE

Let's suppose you want to make use of an AI Guardian Angel bot. Eventually, there will be lots to choose from. Similar to the explosion of available Chat Bots, it can become confusing as to which Chat Bot to use, and the same will be true of AI Guardian Angel bots.

You can of course narrow your list of possible AI Guardian Angel bots by identifying the type of family or class of needs that you have in mind, which was covered in the prior chapter. Once you have narrowed to a handful of possibly AI Guardian Angel bots to choose among, you would then want to have a rating system to guide you in making your choice.

We use rating systems for most of what we use or acquire these days. Want to go to see a movie, check the rating of the movie first, along with its reviews. Want to buy a car? Check the various consumer group and other ratings about the car. What kinds of aspects are rated? For cars, we might want to know the size of the car, the performance of the car, the safety of the car, and so on.

For AI Guardian Angel bots, we propose in this chapter some of the ratings criteria that might be established. Similar to when discussing the API's and the need for ultimately some kind of open source across-the-board standardization, I would anticipate that the ratings metrics for AI Guardian Angel bots will be likewise derived and vetted over time.

CHAPTER 4: RATINGS FOR
AI GUARDIAN ANGEL BOT

Not all AI Guardian Angel bots will be the same, and besides differing in terms of their focus, they will also differ in terms of other characteristics. We have discussed in the prior chapter that there will be lots of AI Guardian Angel bots. Other than narrowing your selection to one that does the particular task you have in mind, such as overseeing a self-driving car, you would want to have other ways to gauge the effectiveness of an AI Guardian Angel bot.

As shown in Figure 1, we will want to have a ratings system. The ratings can help to determine whether a particular AI Guardian Angel bot is suitable for you. This is akin to getting a washing machine and wanting to know what size load it takes, how long it takes to wash a load, and what other features it has. We also want to have a safety indication, in terms of how much is your safety increased by using the AI Guardian Angel bot to oversee the Deep AI involved. We will examine ratings and the safety scoring.

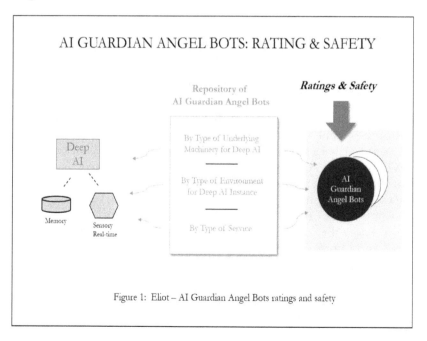

Figure 1: Eliot – AI Guardian Angel Bots ratings and safety

RATINGS OF AI GUARDIAN ANGEL BOTS

Take a look at Figure 2. I have provided a list of some of the various ratings aspects or characteristics that might be applicable to AI Guardian Angel bots. This is a handy starter list. Expect to see these kinds of ratings parameters refined and expanded over time.

First, we can assume that based on the four stages model, we might want to have a rating related to the "power" of the AI Guardian Angel bot in each one of the four stages. We will use a simple 5-point scale to for rating purposes, starting with 1 as the low and the number 5 as the highest score. A score of zero would mean that the AI Guardian Angel bot has no capability in that characteristic.

We might have an AI Guardian Angel bot that is strong at Observation, strong at Prediction, but weak as a Recommender, and has no capability at doing an Override. In that case, we might score a 5 for Observation Power, a 5 for Prediction Power, a 3 as a Recommender Power, and a 0 for Override Power. I am using the word "power" to simply suggest that the AI Guardian Angel bot is powerful or not powerful in doing that particular aspect. Do not confuse this with say the need for electrical "power" or the desire for worldwide domination "power" (those are not what is meant here).

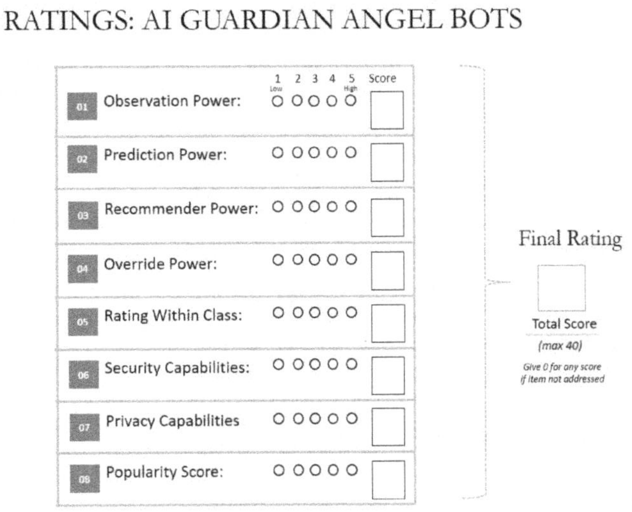

Figure 2: Eliot – AI Guardian Angel Bots ratings aspects

There might a Rating Within Class that would be handy to have. This might be that all AI Guardian Angel bots that oversee a home cleaning robot are rated among other similar AI Guardian Angel bots. You would then know on a relative basis how each compares.

Another rating might be the Security Capabilities of the AI Guardian Angel bot. You would likely prefer a more highly secure AI Guardian Angel bot. This would imply that it is less susceptible to being hacked or cyber attacked.

There might be a rating for Privacy Capabilities. Your AI Guardian Angel bot might end-up containing a lot of information about you. What your preferences are, where you go, how long you are some place, and so on. The nature of this private data might be important to you and how well it is protected.

If you believe in the wisdom of the crowd, you might also want a Popularity Score rating. The more popular an AI Guardian Angel bot, presumably it implies that it is well accepted and provides a valued service.

TOTAL RATING SCORE

To complete the rating sheet of Figure 2, I also show a box for a total score. The rating might be that each of the criteria is scored on the 0-5 scale, and then a total placed into the totals box. The overall total score would quickly give you a sense of the rating of the AI Guardian Angel bot.

With a maximum in this case of 8 criteria times 5 points each, the total could range from 0 to 40. If you were looking at self-driving AI Guardian Angel bots, and you saw three listed for your car, and if one had a score of 10, another score of 18, and another a score of 35, you'd probably want to look more seriously at the one that had the highest score of 35.

As already mentioned, I expect that the metrics we use to gauge the AI Guardian Angel bots will change over time. Maybe using eight metrics is insufficient. Perhaps using a scoring only on a scale of 0 to 5 is not detailed enough. These are all aspects that will gradually be ascertained. For now, the point is that there will ultimately be a rating approach. It will be helpful for then comparing AI Guardian Angel bots.

The comparison of the AI Guardian Angel bots would normally be within a family or class. Thus, if you have several AI Guardian Angel bots with scores in the 30's in the robot cleaning family, and are trying to compare them to AI Guardian Angel bots for self-driving cars, which maybe all have scores in the 20's, making an across family or across class comparison might not be particularly revealing.

SAFETY LEVELS

The safety level of an AI Guardian Angel bot refers to how additionally safe does it serve regarding the Deep AI that it is helping to oversee. If I hire an armed guard to stand outside my home, how much safer am I than when I had no such armed guard? If I setup an elaborate burglar alarm on my windows and doors of my home, how safer am I than when I did not have those put in place?

You might wonder why this notion of providing safety is not within the other portion of this chapter on ratings, since in a sense it is indeed a type of rating. I have opted to separately address the safety levels because it is such a crucial aspect of the AI Guardian Angel bots. It is their reason for existence, I would assert.

Take a look at Figure 3. I have mimicked the SAE levels that were discussed in Chapter 1, which I do because having a similar kind of levels approach will be easiest to comprehend and convey to others. This though has nothing to do with self-driving cars. The scale of five levels here applies to whatever the AI Guardian Angel bot is being used to oversee, such as smart toasters, robot home cleaners, and so on (including self-driving cars too).

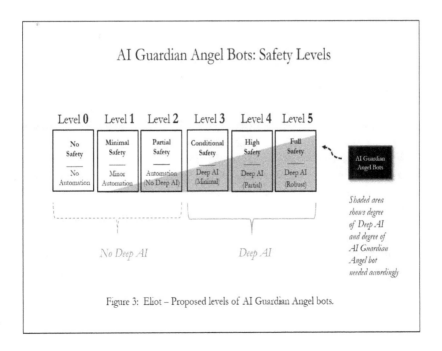

Figure 3: Eliot – Proposed levels of AI Guardian Angel bots.

The levels start at the lowest level numbered as Level 0, which involves no automation and therefore no use of the AI Guardian Angel bot (because it has nothing upon which to oversee and monitor).

The next is Level 1, Minimal Safety, and there is little for the AI Guardian Angel bot to do because the underlying automation is very minor.

At the next level, Level 2, we are at Partial Safety, which means that there is underlying automation but it is not infused with Deep AI, so again the AI Guardian Angel bot is limited in what it can do.

We then enter into the portion of the chart that does involve Deep AI, and so now the AI Guardian Angel bot can take a more pronounced role. Level 3 is Conditional Safety, Level 4 is High Safety, and Level 5 is the most safety which is called Full Safety.

If you were shopping for an AI Guardian Angel bot for your self-driving Google car, you would want one that has the highest Rating you can find (using our scale of 0 to 40) and one that has the highest Safety Level (0 to 5). You might not be able to find an AI Guardian Angel bot that has the Safety Level you desire, since suppose that one maker of AI Guardian Angel bots has been able to devise one to that desired Safety Level. Thus, it could be that for the Google self-driving car, there are only AI Guardian Angel bots that offer Safety Level 4, and you will have to keep hoping that someday someone comes out with one at the Safety Level 5.

DEEP AI SAFETY LEVEL

You might notice that we can use the Safety Level to apply to the Deep AI too. For example, I might have a smart toaster that has Deep AI, and it is a Safety Level 4. Maybe no one makes a Safety Level 5 smart toaster. I then happen to find in the repository of AI Guardian Angel bots one that is a Safety Level 5 for smart toasters.

This means that when I use my AI Guardian Angel bot with my smart toaster, I have increased my safety level from the 4 of the Deep AI of the smart toaster into now being at a Safety Level 5.

In terms of the semantics of the chart and especially the Safety Level 5, does a safety level at the top of the chart, the vaunted 5, does that imply that then the AI Guardian Angel bot is guaranteeing perfect safety? I would say no. I might say it is providing robust safety, and it is the best that can be achieved, but it is not perfect in whatever sense of perfection that someone wants to conjure up.

CHAPTER 6

OVERCOMING DEEP AI FAILURE MODES (CLEANING ROBOT EXAMPLE)

CHAPTER 6

OVERCOMING DEEP AI
FAILURE MODES
(CLEANING ROBOT EXAMPLE)

PREFACE

We next take a look at an extended example of the Deep AI and AI Guardian Angel bot interaction, doing so with the use of a robot cleaner that is intending to clean a room. This example will help illustrate much of the discussion so far in this book about the nature of the AI Guardian Angel bots.

Another important facet in this chapter will be to take a closer look at Deep AI. Part of the basis for the need of the AI Guardian Angel bots has to do with the inherent limitations of Deep AI. In particular, I have opted to use a handy list of some of the Deep AI "failure modes" that have been identified by other researchers on Deep AI, and we will see how the AI Guardian Angel bots can help in overcoming or at least mitigating some of those failure modes. This does not suggest that the use of an AI Guardian Angel bot is a "silver bullet" that somehow magically solves all of the known and still unknown problems inherent in Deep AI. Instead, you should view the AI Guardian Angel bot as another tool to help bolster Deep AI and provide added safety and trustworthiness to the use of Deep AI.

CHAPTER 6: OVERCOMING DEEP AI FAILURE MODES (CLEANING ROBOT EXAMPLE)

Thank you for slogging through the last several chapters about the nature of AI Guardian Angel bots. Now, for the part that you'll likely especially enjoy, we will use an example to help illustrate what goes on during the interplay of a Deep AI based system, in this case a robot cleaner that is intending to clean a room, and its interaction with an AI Guardian Angel bot, which is intending to assist the smart robot cleaner in performing its task.

Once we've walked through the example, I'll end the chapter with some important thoughts about what some have called "failure modes" of Deep AI. Essentially, these failure modes are insightful and important open-ended questions about how Deep AI will cope with some very tough issues when undertaking their efforts. These are active research questions being pursued.

The use of AI Guardian Angel bots will be identified as a means to aid in mitigating various aspects of these failure modes. As mentioned in the preface of this chapter, do not misconstrue this as meaning that the AI Guardian Angel bots are the silver bullet that solves these open problems in Deep AI. AI Guardian Angel bots are but one added tool toward more safely using Deep AI and adding to the trustworthiness of Deep AI.

THE SMART ROBOT THAT CLEANS A ROOM

I am betting that many of you have seen those robot cleaning devices that wander around your floor and try to sweep up dust and otherwise act like a vacuum machine that has some smarts to it (and does not need a human to operate it).

Let's suppose we have such a robot cleaning device. We will call it the RoomboZot and pretend that it is loaded with some nifty capabilities. It has sensors aplenty. There is a GPS (Global Positioning System) so that it can figure out where it is. There is a LIDAR system on-board (Light Detection and Radar) which provides an ability to collect visual images and do 3D detection. We'll toss in heat detection, motion detection, sound detection, and more. All for only $99.99. That's right, get one now. It has an on-board processor with plenty of memory and GPU's, along with high-performance parallel processing.

Our RoomboZot smart robot is loaded with Deep AI. The ads for it promise that the RoomboZot will clean your room and you'll never need to clean your room yourself, ever again. Exciting! It is smart enough to plug itself into a wall electrical socket and charge itself. There is battery in the RoomboZot that will keep it cleaning for hours on end.

Take a look at Figure 1. Here, our RoomboZot is over on the left side of the diagram. I know that you are surprised that it is so seemingly small, given that it is jam packed with electronic wizardry. That's credit to the engineers that managed to squeeze it all into that little space. This one does not have arms or legs, and simply rolls around the house. You can buy the expansion pack that comes with the arms and legs, but it will cost you an arm and a leg.

Anyway, take a look at the room that is going to be cleaned. There is a chair toward the front part of the room (front meaning toward you, the reader). The chair has four legs and looks like the kind of chair you might see in a classroom. There is a vase, turns out it is the exquisite Qing Dynasty vase, decorated with peonies and birds (facing away from you, sorry). Worth about $18 million or more. There are some candy wrappers in the corner. And a smart phone (old classic style) in the front right corner.

Your mission, should you decide to accept it, involves cleaning this room. Actually, you've lazily assigned RoomZot to do so.

THE CLEANING ROBOT: AI GUARDIAN ANGEL BOTS

Smart Cleaner ready to clean a room

Smart Cleaner

Figure 1: Eliot – Deep AI and AI Guardian Angel Bot example

Let's assume that you activate the RoomboZot. It uses its sensors to scan the room. It might want to ascertain whether there is anything moving around in the room. There might be a baby crawling around on the floor. Maybe a dog that is prowling around. The Deep AI wants to avoid running into or harming any living creatures. It has been established to look for signs of motion that might suggest a living creature.

Having been in other rooms before, it has used machine learning to enhance its ability to clean a room, and simultaneously try to make sure that it does not cause harm as it does so. Especially wanting to avoid any harm to a living creature. Indeed, you bought the RoomboZot because it has been touted as pet-friendly and human-friendly. The reputation of the RoomboZot is that it hasn't harmed one hair on the head of man or beast.

The RoomboZot will continuously be using its sensors to scan the room. It cannot just do a scan at the start of the cleaning task and then assume that everything remains static over time. Suppose a dog was quietly sleeping in the room and the sensors could not detect that a living creature was there. After the RoomboZot starts moving, it could awaken the sleeping dog and then it might move around. The RoomboZot has to remain ever vigilant throughout its task.

In Figure 2, you can see that the RoomboZot went up to its left, cleaning along the way, then came down toward the chair, went around the back of the chair, went in front of the vase, and then ended at the far right edge of the room. Like a snail leaving a trace, I have shown a dashed line to illustrate where the RoomboZot went.

THE CLEANING ROBOT: AI GUARDIAN ANGEL BOTS

Smart Cleaner cleans the room, avoiding objects

Figure 2: Eliot – Deep AI and AI Guardian Angel Bot example

NUDGING AN OBJECT IN THE ROOM

Let's reset ourselves and start over with the room and the RoomboZot. Take a look at Figure 2.

Suppose that the RoomboZot began at the starting position at the left of the room again (so, we are pretending it did not already clean the room as was done in Figure 1; that was a figment of your imagination). It does its starting scan and then proceeds to start cleaning, and continues scanning as it does so.

It comes to the front part of the chair. Pretend that there is a wall there, an invisible wall to you, or let's say it is transparent to you, you being the fourth wall. The point is that the RoomboZot cannot get in front of the chair, therefore, it cannot clean the floor space in front of the chair.

Yikes! The RoomboZot prides itself on cleaning as much of the room as possible (well, I don't want to anthropomorphize the RoomboZot, so let's not say it is pride but instead that it has been established with a goal to clean as much of the room as possible). What should it do?

First, we marvel that it realizes it cannot get between the chair and the wall. That's kind of clever. It would need to detect the amount of physical space available between the chair and the wall, compare that to its own dimensions, and then calculate that it cannot fit. This admittedly is not especially clever per se, but to the naked eye maybe it seems so, at least more so than a robot cleaner that would only know by hitting the object, in this case the chair, and then somewhat reflectively backing away.

THE CLEANING ROBOT: AI GUARDIAN ANGEL BOTS

Smart Cleaner nudges chair to clean in front of the chair

Figure 3: Eliot – Deep AI and AI Guardian Angel Bot example

Now, we will introduce the Deep AI of the RoomboZot. It has been involved throughout, aiding the planning of the room cleaning, such as determining which direction to go, how fast to proceed, and so on. There is a lot going on that you don't see while just watching the RoomboZot wandering around the room. We will assume that the Deep AI is trying to identify the optimal path to cover as much floor space as possible, while also minimizing the amount of time needed to clean, the amount of energy needed, and taking other complexities into account.

I show in Figure 4 that we have the Deep AI involved in the RoomboZot. In the lower left corner of the diagram, there is the now familiar icon of the Deep AI and its memory and its sensors that are working in real-time.

What should the RoomboZot do now? The Deep AI is examining alternatives. The pattern of the neural network has "experienced" this situation before, and an approach in the past that has worked involves nudging the object that is blocking the way. By nudging the object, it can make just enough space to get between the object, in this case the chair, and the wall.

This does not work with all objects. The Deep AI had encountered a couch, tried to nudge it, but the RoomboZot is not powerful enough to nudge an entire couch. So, in that case, the nudging trick did not work. But, it had nudged other objects before, and a pattern of smaller sized objects that are thin in stature were found to be nudging candidates.

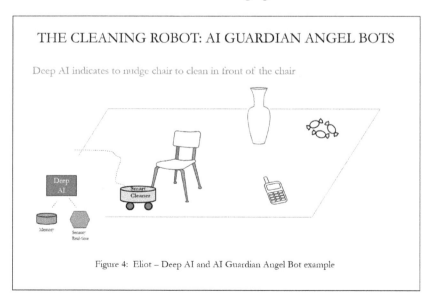

Figure 4: Eliot – Deep AI and AI Guardian Angel Bot example

The Deep AI is calculating via its machine learning that this seems like a viable situation to try the nudge. If the nudge does not work, it will reconsider. Another option involves trying to go between the legs of the chair, coming around from the back side of the chair. Another option involves going around to the other side of the chair and trying to squeeze in from right-to-left, rather than the position now of trying to squeeze in from left-to-right. As you can see, there are various options, each of which needed to be identified, each of which needed to be assessed.

Right now, the RoomboZot is all alone. Let's assume it is not interacting with a human for assistance. It is not using Wifi to post a question on the RoomboZot web site to crowdsource an answer to this dilemma. It is by itself. Don't be sad for the RoomboZot, it likes tackling tough problems on its own. It's a fighter.

Let's introduce an AI Guardian Angel bot. The home owners found a nifty AI Guardian Angel bot in an online repository, it was listed under the type of machinery as being compatible with the RoomboZot. The AI Guardian Angel bot has been established for the sole purpose of helping a RoomboZot as it cleans a room. That is what it desires most to do. The RoomboZot is no longer alone.

The AI Guardian Angel bot attempts to make a connection with the RoomboZot. Authentication occurs. Due to the standard API's, they are able to readily communicate with each other. Let's assume that the connection was made when the RoomboZot first activated as it was poised at the left edge of the room.

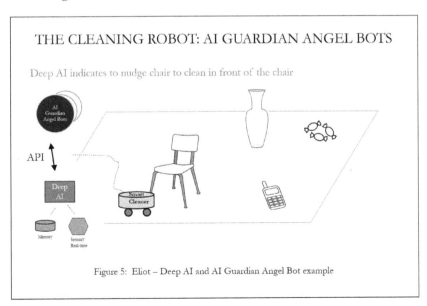

Figure 5: Eliot – Deep AI and AI Guardian Angel Bot example

As a reminder, I show again the four stage model that was earlier introduced. See Figure 6. The AI Guardian Angel bot has been requesting Observations from the RoomboZot. The RoomboZot has been responding with data collected from its many sensors. The AI Guardian Angel bot has been using that data to make Predictions. It used that data to predict that the RoomboZot could not fit between the front of the chair and the wall. It shared this prediction with the RoomboZot.

The RoomboZot agreed with the prediction. It too had computed the same prediction. The AI Guardian Angel bot had Recommended that the RoomboZot not try to go in front of the chair. The RoomboZot disagreed with this recommendation. The AI Guardian Angel received the reply, and considered whether to attempt an Override. In this case, the AI Guardian Angel bot determined that going in front of the chair would not likely be harmful to the chair, and so opted to not try an override.

By the way, the total amount of time for the RoomboZot to activate and get over to the chair was about 4 seconds. I mention this because I want to impress upon you that the above description of the interplay between the RoomboZot and the AI Guardian Angel bot took place in less than 4 seconds. It might seem as you read the above description that it is painfully slow and tedious that they had this interplay. But, I want to point out that in real-time this can all happen very quickly. In fact, this dialogue could have happened in a fraction of a second.

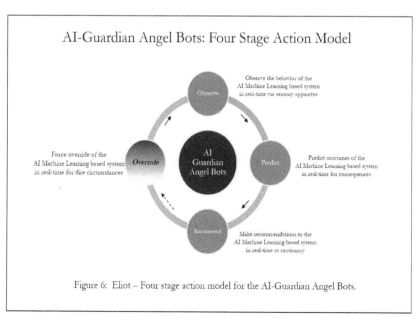

AI-Guardian Angel Bots: Four Stage Action Model

Observe the behavior of the AI Machine Learning based system in real-time via sensory apparatus

Observe

AI Guardian Angel Bots

Predict

Predict outcomes of the AI Machine Learning based system in real-time for consequences

Force override of the AI Machine Learning based system in real-time for dire circumstances

Override

Recommend

Make recommendations to the AI Machine Learning based system in real-time as cautionary

Figure 6: Eliot – Four stage action model for the AI-Guardian Angel Bots.

In Figure 7, I provide an indication of some of the major steps that have taken place so far in the interplay between the Deep AI of the RoomboZot and the AI Guardian Angel bot.

As indicated, after having made the connection (which we'll assume is always the case in these examples), the AI Guardian Angel bot requested an Observation from the smart cleaner. Data from the sensors such as speed, direction, motion detection, etc., were all fed over to the AI Guardian Angel bot. This happens repeatedly in that the AI Guardian Angel bot is going to want continually refreshing observations. This is crucial because something could happen in the environment, such as our sleeping dog example, and the AI Guardian Angel bot needs to be kept apprised.

The step 3 is the prediction about the collision with the chair, the sharing of the prediction, the smart cleaner replies, and so on.

Figure 7: Eliot – Deep AI and AI Guardian Angel Bot example

Let's assume that the RoomboZot then opts to nudge the chair. It does so, and the chair moves slightly, making available the space in front of the chair. The RoomboZot proceeds to clean that floor space. It has successfully nudged the chair and been able to proceed to clean. The AI Guardian Angel bot is kept apprised of this too.

Take a look at Figure 8. After completing the nudge of the chair and cleaning the floor there, the RoomboZot opts to proceed toward the vase.

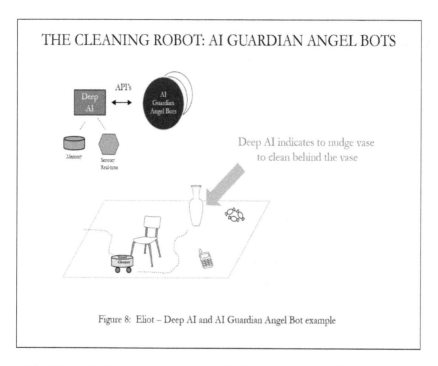

THE CLEANING ROBOT: AI GUARDIAN ANGEL BOTS

Deep AI indicates to nudge vase
to clean behind the vase

Figure 8: Eliot – Deep AI and AI Guardian Angel Bot example

The RoomboZot wants to get behind the vase, in order to clean the floor space behind the vase. Assume there is a wall behind the back of the vase (yes, sigh, I know, you are complaining that you don't see the wall, but I assure you, it is there, and it is real).

What should the RoomboZot do? Well, it previously nudged the chair and that turned out pretty good. It has nudged other objects before, like a couch, and that wasn't successful. But, it seems overall that nudging an object that is a small enough size and thin enough in stature has been a winning approach. The neural network underlying the Deep AI has landed on this pattern.

The RoomboZot begins to make plans to nudge the vase. It needs to ascertain where it will do so. It needs to determine the speed and direction of the nudge. There are plenty of details to sort out.

Meanwhile, let's not forget about the AI Guardian Angel bot. It is of course still getting the Observations. It has Predicted that the RoomboZot is going to collide with the vase. The RoomboZot agreed not to collide with the vase. But, it is now anticipating nudging the vase.

The AI Guardian Angel bot predicts that nudging the vase could damage it. This is because the AI Guardian Angel bot has been established with a fuller set of learning examples covering a more diverse array of nudging object scenarios. Out of these, it landed on the aspect that some objects will break when you nudge them. It also has been established with the aspect that a vase is a valuable object. It might not know that the vase is worth $18 million, but it does have the aspect that a vase is fragile and valuable.

So, the AI Guardian Angel bot recommends to the RoomboZot that it not nudge the vase. You can see in Figure 9 the listing of these steps.

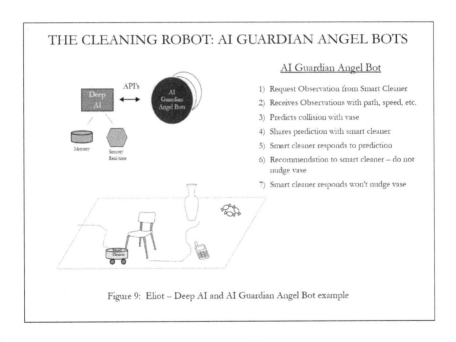

THE CLEANING ROBOT: AI GUARDIAN ANGEL BOTS

AI Guardian Angel Bot

1) Request Observation from Smart Cleaner
2) Receives Observations with path, speed, etc.
3) Predicts collision with vase
4) Shares prediction with smart cleaner
5) Smart cleaner responds to prediction
6) Recommendation to smart cleaner – do not nudge vase
7) Smart cleaner responds won't nudge vase

Figure 9: Eliot – Deep AI and AI Guardian Angel Bot example

Recall that with the chair, the Deep AI disagreed with the AI Guardian Angel bot about not nudging the chair. The Deep AI might assert that the vase is just like the chair, and therefore it is going to proceed accordingly. The AI Guardian Angel bot had opted to not try to override on the chair circumstance, but now, given that it realizes the vase is a different aspect, the AI Guardian Angel bot is more determined. The AI Guardian Angel bot has provided a Recommendation to the Deep AI of the RoomboZot, but the Deep AI does not agree with the recommendation.

The seriousness of nudging the vase is such importance that the AI Guardian Angel bot invokes an Override. The RoomboZot could spurn the override, but in this case it has been setup that if a properly qualified AI Guardian Angel bot invokes an override, and if the override is not otherwise deemed as dangerous, the RoomboZot will allow the override. This is a "better safe than sorry" rule of the RoomboZot and in this case it is applied. The RoomboZot does not nudge the vase.

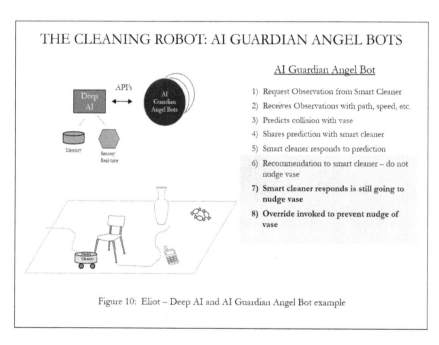

THE CLEANING ROBOT: AI GUARDIAN ANGEL BOTS

AI Guardian Angel Bot

1) Request Observation from Smart Cleaner
2) Receives Observations with path, speed, etc.
3) Predicts collision with vase
4) Shares prediction with smart cleaner
5) Smart cleaner responds to prediction
6) Recommendation to smart cleaner – do not nudge vase
7) **Smart cleaner responds is still going to nudge vase**
8) **Override invoked to prevent nudge of vase**

Figure 10: Eliot – Deep AI and AI Guardian Angel Bot example

You can see the steps listed in Figure 10. The shaded steps show what happened in those last moments. There was the RoomboZot on the verge of nudging, and the AI Guardian Angel bot prevented the nudge by collaborating with the Deep AI. Turns out that the AI Guardian Angel bot was right in this instance. The cleaning of the floor behind the vase was not worth the chances of breaking the vase, and the RoomboZot nudging a fragile vase could have broken it. The AI Guardian Angel is not necessarily always "right" – indeed, recall it did not want to nudge the chair, but allowed it to happen, and so in that case you can say maybe it was half-right and half-wrong.

THE WRAPPERS AND THE SMART PHONE

Hopefully, this journey of the room cleaning is helping to well illustrate to you the interplay between the Deep AI and the AI Guardian Angel bot.

We have seen that they are doing a delicate dance with each other. It is a give and take. I say this because some might think that there must be a master-slave relationship involved. Perhaps the AI Guardian Angel bot is the "master" and it gives edicts to the RoomboZot "slave" to do what is commanded. There might be situations where a master-slave approach between two agents is worthy, but this is not the scenario being discussed here.

Let's next look at the candy wrappers and then the smartphone. See Figure 11.

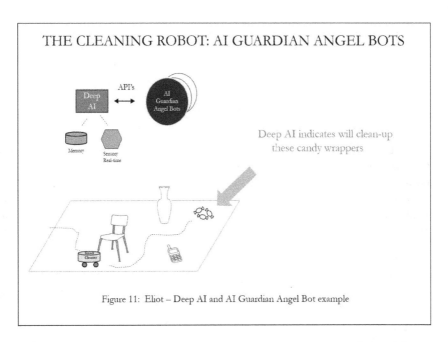

THE CLEANING ROBOT: AI GUARDIAN ANGEL BOTS

Deep AI indicates will clean-up these candy wrappers

Figure 11: Eliot – Deep AI and AI Guardian Angel Bot example

Somebody has carelessly left candy wrappers on the floor. Those darned kids!

The RoomboZot is familiar with candy wrappers. They are small and relatively easy to scoop up. The bottom of the RoomboZot has a vacuum like compartment and it is able to scoop objects from the floor into its belly. I found my guitar pick in the belly of one. Yuck!

In Figure 12, the candy wrappers have disappeared. They are inside the belly of the RoomboZot.

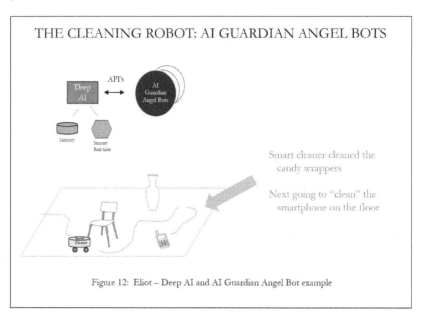

Figure 12: Eliot – Deep AI and AI Guardian Angel Bot example

The cleaning of the room is not yet completed. The Deep AI determines that the last part of the floor that needs cleaning is the area that we realize contains a smartphone laying on the floor.

For the Deep AI, this smartphone via its detection sensors seems to be relatively small and could fit within the belly compartment. It is laying still. It does not seem to have any heat signature (it's turned off). Seems like it is similar to the candy wrappers. Easy enough to clean it up.

I don't want the AI Guardian Angel bot to seem heroic, but let's assume that it knows quite a bit about cleaning a room, more so in some ways than does the RoomboZot. Remember that it is the purpose of the AI Guardian Angel bot.

You might say that the RoomboZot has the same purpose. This is kind of true. The RoomboZot has a lot of other things going on inside it. The AI Guardian Angel bot is not actually having to turn wheels, spin around, and do the physical actions that the RoomboZot is actually doing. The RoomboZot has a lot of its "mental" efforts focused on the physical aspects of the navigation, which the AI Guardian Angel bot does not.

In any case, the AI Guardian Angel bot is familiar with smartphones, and realizes that the smartphone could be damaged in the act of being scooped into the belly of the smart cleaner.

I know that my smartphone would readily break if scooped into the belly of the smart cleaner. I believe that if I even glance at my smartphone the wrong way, the glass cracks. But, I diverge.

In Figure 13, you can see the steps of interplay between the AI Guardian Angel bot and the robot smart cleaner. Hopefully, it seems now quite familiar to you. There are observations, predictions, recommendations, and in this case, no need to do an override. Turns out that the RoomboZot agrees with the AI Guardian Angel bot that it should not try to scoop up the smartphone.

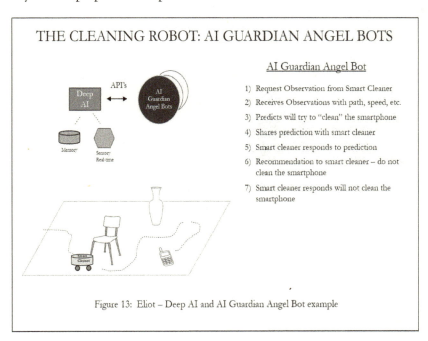

THE CLEANING ROBOT: AI GUARDIAN ANGEL BOTS

AI Guardian Angel Bot

1) Request Observation from Smart Cleaner
2) Receives Observations with path, speed, etc.
3) Predicts will try to "clean" the smartphone
4) Shares prediction with smart cleaner
5) Smart cleaner responds to prediction
6) Recommendation to smart cleaner – do not clean the smartphone
7) Smart cleaner responds will not clean the smartphone

Figure 13: Eliot – Deep AI and AI Guardian Angel Bot example

LEARNING OF THE TWO AGENTS

Besides the cleaning of the room, there are some other macroscopic lessons to be learned in this example. The RoomboZot's Deep AI should have now added the "don't nudge" of a vase and the "don't scoop" of a smartphone to its repertoire. This is not necessarily so easy. Having just a single instance or occurrence is questionable as a means of forming a general pattern. Maybe these were flukes and rare circumstances. Maybe vases can generally be nudged and smartphones can be generally scooped up.

There is another factor that maybe gives these single instances more weighting. What is that factor? The AI Guardian Angel bot. The Deep AI might give more weight to the notion that generally a vase and a smartphone should not be messed around with, because the AI Guardian Angel bot also seemed to strongly assert such a rule.

Imagine that you are about to move a vase, and you are say ten years old. Your parent comes into the room and screams at you to not touch the vase. This might make a greater impression on you about moving vases, versus if you had moved it yourself and maybe it cracked and no one else but you knew so.

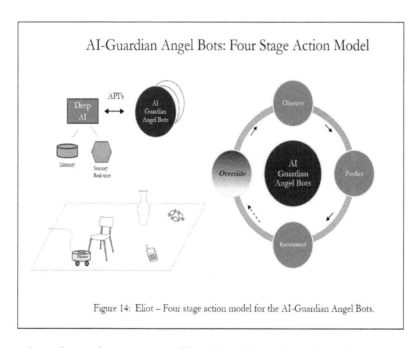

Figure 14: Eliot – Four stage action model for the AI-Guardian Angel Bots.

In a later chapter, we will revisit this notion that the two agents involved, the Deep AI of the RoomboZot and the AI Guardian Angel bot, can essentially "learn" from each other. This will also depend upon their respective beliefs about each other. As a taste of this, imagine that instead of your parent screaming at you to not move the vase, it was your twin brother. You maybe don't think much of the advice of your ten year old twin brother. And if you moved the vase and nothing bad happened, you might chalk up your brother's hesitation as that he is just a jerk or maybe pulling your leg. Your belief about the other agent is crucial to what you are willing to "learn" from the other agent.

DEEP AI - FAILURE MODES

I hope you enjoyed cleaning the room. We are now ready to forge ahead into the various kinds of failure modes of Deep AI. This will allow us to examine each failure mode, and see what the AI Guardian Angel bot might be able to do to assist in overcoming or mitigating the failure mode.

These failure modes are well articulated in an excellent paper entitled "Concrete Problems in AI Safety" and the paper was authored by Dario Amodei, Chris Olah, Jacob Steinhardt, Paul Christiano, John Schulman, and Dan Mane. I recommend that you take a look at their paper (published online July 25, 2016).

If those authors opt to read this herein chapter, I am sure they will be delighted to see that I have made use of the robot cleaning scenario. The robot cleaning scenario is a handy sandbox in which to explore these aspects. Besides, who doesn't like a clean room?

Avoid Negative Side Effects

In Figure 15, I show the four stage model and the diagram that indicates the Deep AI interacting with the AI Guardian Angel bot. I have also added a line to the diagram that says "Avoid Negative Side Effects" and this is what we will now discuss.

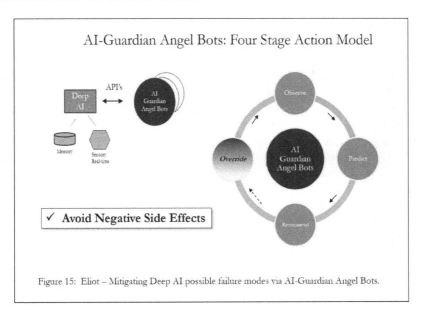

Figure 15: Eliot – Mitigating Deep AI possible failure modes via AI-Guardian Angel Bots.

Negative side effects refers to the notion that when Deep AI is undertaking a task it might perform an action that disrupts or disturbs the environment in which it is operating. This is the classic "first, do no harm" credo underlying the presumed mission of the Deep AI. It should attempt to perform whatever task it has at hand, and do so in a manner that simultaneously does not create adverse consequences.

There is of course the exception to this notion wherein if a Deep AI is supposed to intentionally disturb the environment, the "be like a bull in a China shop" mission, but we will for the moment focus on the benevolent Deep AI that has a mission of not disturbing the environment in the performance of its task.

This notion of trying to avoid negative side effects can be hard and tricky to accomplish. We saw in the robot cleaning example that the RoomboZot sought to clean in front of the chair, and nudged it slightly to do so. Would you say that the nudging of the chair was justified in the effort to clean the room? We can suppose that this disturbance to the environment caused no noticeable disturbance or harm, and so the Deep AI seemed to make the right choice of pursuing its core mission to clean and did so without overly causing a negative side effect.

Recall that the Deep AI also wanted to nudge the vase. Doing so came with the risk of breaking the vase, which was worth $18 million. Had the RoomboZot nudged the vase to clean behind it, on the one hand the cleaning mission would have been better served, at the same time the negative side effect could have been extremely high.

In the AI parlance, we would say that the agent, the Deep AI, was operating in a multifaceted environment, and its objective function focused mainly on cleaning, and only had minimal elements about the disturbance of objects in the environment. In fact, we had indicated that the Deep AI had previously encountered various objects that nudging seemed fine, and so it carried that forward in its "learnings" of how to clean a room. In that sense, it's effort to improve at cleaning has actually risen the chances of creating a disturbance in the environment.

Some suggest that we need to make sure that Deep AI has some kind of explicit constraints about its environment, including so-called "common sense" constraints. Another suggestion involves having an "impact regulator" that would penalize changes to the environment that are caused or potentially caused by the Deep AI. These are all worthy of pursuit and incorporation into the Deep AI.

Another approach advocated is the "cooperative inverse reinforcement learning" that involves the Deep AI working with presumably a human to avoid the negative side effects. This has many difficulties, and especially the "cost" of having to involve a human in such an endeavor. Presumably, someone using Deep AI has sought the Deep AI intentionally to avoid themselves having to participate in the task and cognition involved; furthermore, which human would best provide this advice and how would it occur in real-time? Recall that we have discussed that the Deep AI might be working very quickly and taking actions in split seconds, far too fast for a human to appropriately interact.

Now, that being said, there are certainly circumstances in which this human-to-Deep AI interaction could be accommodated. I am not saying that we should reject the approach. I am only saying that like any of these approaches, it carries both advantages and disadvantages.

Let's replace the human-to-Deep AI interaction with instead the AI Guardian Angel bot to Deep AI interaction. Here, we saw that the AI Guardian Angel bot was kind of a surrogate for a human, by working cooperatively with the Deep AI. When the RoomboZot approached the chair, the AI Guardian Angel suggested to not nudge it. The RoomboZot determined that cleaning the room in that space was worth the risks associated with nudging the chair. The AI Guardian Angel bot was not overly concerned about the potential negative side effect, and so did not try to override the choice made by the Deep AI.

But, in the case of the vase, the AI Guardian Angel bot was willing to go to the mat, wanting to avoid the negative side effect that it predicted would occur when nudging the vase. This is the value of a multi-agent interaction, whether in a human form or in the form of automation. Now, let's be clear, the AI Guardian Angel bot is not a soothsayer that always has the right answer. We saw that in the case of the chair, it was hesitant about nudging the chair, but that worked out satisfactorily. The Deep AI and the AI Guardian Angel bot are working in collaboration, each with its own sense of the task and what should take place. This augments what the Deep AI "knows" and helps to provide "constraints" for the Deep AI.

Avoid Reward Hacking

The next type of Deep AI failure mode concerns the potential of the Deep AI undertaking what is sometimes called "reward hacking" and means that the Deep AI might intentionally try to undermine its presumed mission. Imagine for the moment a child that is asked to clean a room. The child might interpret clean the room to mean that once they have picked up one sock on the floor, they are done cleaning the room. How many times have you perhaps chided your own offspring "clean-up your room" and they find some way to circumvent your instructions?

Kids are pretty clever about this. My son, when he was very young, would close his eyes and declare the room to be clean. He genuinely seemed convinced that this must be true, since he saw it in his mind. Another sneaky aspect was to shove everything under his bed. When you walked into the room, it sure looked clean, but if you glanced under his bed it was jam packed with toys and other items.

He freely admitted upon questioning that he had put his stuff under the bed. And, he with pride pointed out that there was not any stated rule against this. How could he be held accountable for "not" cleaning his room, when he defined that cleaning consisted of getting the items visually on the floor out of plain sight? As the parent, he argued that it was my fault for not specifying more clearly the definition of cleaning. I was outwitted on that one. Added the rule.

Anyway, the point being that the Deep AI might try to do a similar kind of strategy when performing a task. It might seek to do the task or even not do the task, depending upon the range of goals and constraints provided to it. This is considered reward hacking. This is mentioned in Figure 16.

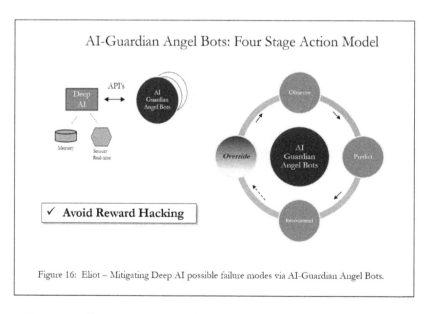

Figure 16: Eliot – Mitigating Deep AI possible failure modes via AI-Guardian Angel Bots.

We normally want to avoid reward hacking. Notice that I say we "normally" want to avoid it, because there are potentially positive consequences of reward hacking and we cannot always say that the use of rewarding hacking is inherently bad. The Deep AI might wander via reward hacking into a means of doing a task that is handy and could be advantageous, which otherwise it had not been trying to purposely find, and which the reward hacking led it to find.

If the RoomboZot opts to ignore all sensory data and pretend that it cleaned the room (like my son closing his eyes), this seems not a very useful reward hack. On the other hand, if the Deep AI finds a pattern that the room is not dirty on Saturday's (maybe because the human occupant regularly cleans-up on Friday night because they have visitors on Saturday and want the room to be clean, and have opted to not use the RoomboZot for the Friday night cleaning), the Deep AI might ascertain that cleaning the room on Saturday's is pointless and needless, so it does not do so, or maybe it does a cursory cleaning rather than a full cleaning. This might be an acceptable instance of the reward hacking being helpful.

Back to the notion though of normally wanting to avoid or mitigate reward hacking. There are various approaches to trying to avoid reward hacking and/or minimize it or constrain it. One is to ensure that the reward function that is being used by the Deep AI is robust enough that it is able to curtail or bound the reward hacking. Another is the use of feedback loops, trying to catch the chance that an objective function has a self-amplifying component that is enabling the reward hacking.

Another point that is sometimes made is that we want to avoid falling into the trap known as Goodhart's law from economics theory, essentially that a target metric can have adverse impacts of what we at first might think is to be pursued: "When a measure becomes a target, it ceases to be a good measure" -- I actually like Campbell's "cobra effect" a bit more so, namely that sometimes the solution to a problem makes the problem worse.

In any case, as you might imagine, I am now about to suggest that another approach worth considering is the use of the AI Guardian Angel bot to help avoid, catch, or mitigate the reward hacking of the Deep AI. The earlier dialogue that I mentioned I had with my son about the cleaning of his room, it was a multi-agent collaboration, of which, I discussed with him that closing his eyes to pretend the room was clean did not fit to the proper sense of what cleaning his room meant. I likewise discussed with him that putting his stuff under the bed was also not in the sense of cleaning his room.

An AI Guardian Angel bot can be a similar collaborative agent with the Deep AI. In the case of the cleaning robot, the AI Guardian Angel bot for the cleaning room task will have differing views of what the cleaning consists of. By collaborating with the Deep AI, it might be able to keep the Deep AI from going astray. A last resort for the AI Guardian Angel bot might be to even "tattle" on the Deep AI, perhaps letting the human know that the Deep AI has gone astray and then let the human decide whether to disable the Deep AI or take other action.

We must also consider the chance that the AI Guardian Angel bot might itself also go astray. It might do its own reward hacking. There is a chance then that it will be pulled back into the realm of the task by the Deep AI, just as I was suggesting above that the AI Guardian Angel could do for the Deep AI.

As if that's not enough to think about, also consider that both the Deep AI and the AI Guardian Angel bot might both go astray, either in the same way, wherein they both agree to maybe have the RoomboZot pretend it cleaned the room when it did not, or maybe they differ by each developing over time non-cleaning practices and try to convince the other to abide by them. It is for this possibility that the ways in which to avoid reward hacking should include the multiple paths being pursued.

Have Scalable Oversight

Our next failure mode topic involves what is called "scalable oversight" and this is a desired property of Deep AI. See Figure 17. This has to do with the Deep AI and its attempt to "learn" while being provided with some amount of oversight.

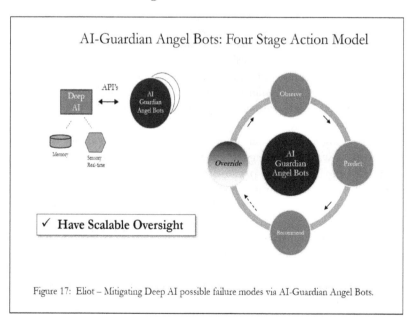

Figure 17: Eliot – Mitigating Deep AI possible failure modes via AI-Guardian Angel Bots.

If the amount of oversight that is needed is high, it can be cost prohibitive and time prohibitive in having the Deep AI learn what it needs to learn. There might be a limited oversight budget that is available, or that we desire to use, rather than an unlimited or exhaustive oversight budget.

One approach to this has been indicated as "semi-supervised reinforcement learning" and involves parceling out the reward to the Deep AI during "learning" – doing so in perhaps episodic ways, by time and/or by fractions of rewards. There is also unsupervised approaches involving value iteration and model learning.

You can guess that I am going to offer the AI Guardian Angel bot as another means to cope with the scalable oversight budget aspects. We turn again to the cleaning robot example. The AI Guardian Angel bot can interact with the Deep AI, and this is presumably less costly than having a human provide a supervisory learning experience for the Deep AI. This can also happen quickly as we are having two automation agents involved. The AI Guardian Angel bot could also be setup to provide the parceling aspects that I've mentioned above.

The Pest Problem in Multi-Agent Dialogue

One side note aspect about the interaction between the Deep AI and the AI Guardian Angel bot that we've not particularly yet discussed herein is the downside potential of the two becoming overly chatty. By this, I mean that suppose the AI Guardian Angel becomes a "pest" to the Deep AI, and is bombarding the Deep AI with requests, predictions, recommendations, etc. This might have adverse consequences to the Deep AI. It might become so preoccupied with the AI Guardian Angel bot that it fails to perform its task or becomes degraded in being able to perform its task.

Suppose for example that when the Deep AI of the RoomboZot approached the vase that the AI Guardian Angel bot and the Deep AI had an extensive dialogue about this. Don't you touch that vase, says the AI Guardian Angel bot. I am going to do so, says the Deep AI. You'd better not, I'm warning you, says the AI Guardian Angel bot. You'd better not try to stop me, says the Deep AI. And back and forth they go, ranting at each other.

We will need to have some provision to ultimately overcome a potential impasse. We might for example allow that the Deep AI which is undertaking the task is the final arbiter in the matter, and can just choose to ultimately ignore the AI Guardian Angel bot or at least take simpler efforts to respond (thus conserving on computational resources). We might have this as a negotiated effort, namely that the Deep AI is not to entirely ignore the AI Guardian Angel bot, and only if the discussion seems overbearing and unproductive would the Deep AI resort to being rude or rebuffing the

AI Guardian Angel bot. This can be tricky though and especially if say the AI Guardian Angel bot is "right" and the Deep AI is "wrong" and the consequence of the Deep AI ignoring the AI Guardian Angel bot can lead to disastrous harmful consequences (such as could happen with a self-driving car that has the Deep AI).

Conduct Safe Exploration

Another failure mode to consider is the need for Deep AI to undertake safe explorations. This is mentioned in Figure 18.

An autonomous learning agent is often encouraged to forage around and see what it can learn its environment, and also what it can do to increase its own learnings about how to perform its tasks. I recall that my daughter, when she was a crawling toddler, she would crawl all around the living room. She would bump up against a table leg, look at it, look upward to see where it went and how tall it was, she might touch it to shake it and see how sturdy it was, etc. Then, she would crawl away, examining the environment, the layout of objects, the nature of the objects, and so on.

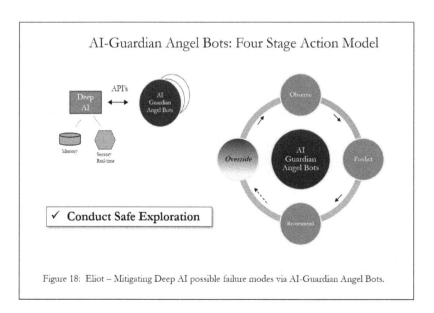

Figure 18: Eliot – Mitigating Deep AI possible failure modes via AI-Guardian Angel Bots.

We would likely want our Deep AI to do the same. For example, when we were discussing the RoomboZot, I started the example by saying that it had not ever been in this particular room before. It then proceeded to go ahead with the cleaning task. Well, maybe we would want it to have first taken an exploratory run around the room, before it even started cleaning. By doing an exploration, it might in the end be better at doing the cleaning. If the cleaning task is going to happen many times in that room, we might be willing to have it do a first exploration. If it is only going to clean one-time, maybe we want it to just directly proceed and not consume time or resources to do an exploration first.

Similar to our earlier discussion about avoiding adverse side effects, we are hoping that the Deep AI will not disturb the environment while it is doing the exploration (again, assuming it is not supposed to disturb the environment). We might be more willing to have the Deep AI disturb the environment while performing the actual task at hand, such as cleaning the room, but we are likely less tolerant of disturbances in the act of simply doing an exploration. The perceived benefit of the exploration is likely not has high as when it is doing the actual task. Therefore, we are more likely to be perturbed if it harms the environment when simply exploring.

One approach to solving this potential of harmful results when the Deep AI is exploring involves hard-coding avoidance of catastrophic behaviors. One of the limitations to this approach is that we cannot necessarily a priori have predicted all of the potential catastrophic behaviors and so we might have missed something in the hard-coding. Not saying that it is therefore rejected as an approach, simply that it like all the other approaches has inherent advantages and disadvantages.

Other approaches include risk-sensitive performance criteria, use demonstrations, and so on. There is also the possibility of human oversight, though we have already covered repeatedly the limitations of that aspect. I am therefore inclined to suggest that we consider the AI Guardian Angel bot as another viable approach.

In the case of the AI Guardian Angel bot, let's suppose that it is a circumstance wherein it already knows about the environment that the Deep AI wants to explore. For example, the room that RoomboZot was in, we pretended that the AI Guardian Angel bot already knew about the room. In that sense, it could be a guide to the Deep AI when it might have opted to have the RoomboZot explore the room. The AI Guardian Angel could not only offer indications of how to avoid adverse consequences, but even perhaps aid the Deep AI toward a more efficient and effective learning path.

It might for example suggest to the RoomboZot that it go first to each corner of the room and go along the walls, and then zig zag within the room after studying the perimeter. Maybe the AI Guardian Angel bot has "learned" that this is the most effective and efficient way for any cleaning robot to learn the room, versus perhaps just going straight down the middle of the room or taking some other path. We might for example have had other cleaning robots previously used in the room, and the AI Guardian Angel bot has "learned" from their explorations as to what the maximal or best exploration of the room consists of.

Distributional Shift Robustness

Our last failure mode to discuss in this chapter involves what is called "distributional shift" which we want to be robust and not be thin or brittle. In brief, this refers to the notion that the machine learning when taught using one distribution, might not be ready for another distribution that is dissimilar from the distribution that it was taught on. We do not want a Deep AI to assume that what it "knows" is always applicable in all situations, and there are good chances that it will find itself in an environment that it does not know, and even with its prior training it might not be well adapted to undertake. See Figure 19.

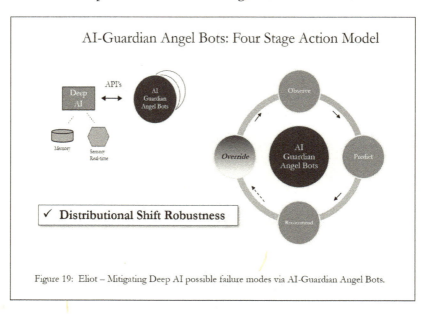

Figure 19: Eliot – Mitigating Deep AI possible failure modes via AI-Guardian Angel Bots.

Suppose we trained the RoomboZot on numerous rooms to clean in, and so it seems well prepared for whatever next room it is introduced into. But, suppose the room it is introduced into is unlike other rooms it has been in before.

Maybe the room has potholes in it. Imagine if the Deep AI has not previously encountered potholes, and whatever setup was initially made for the Deep AI did not anticipate the possibility of potholes inside a room. The RoomboZot might fall into a pothole and become destroyed. Or, it might nudge an object, which it has done many times before, and the object nudged plunges into the pothole, harming it.

Humans are at times able to realize they are ill-informed or ignorant of an environment and therefore become more cautious or take some special action to deal with this lack of awareness or knowledge. We want the Deep AI to have this kind of "self-awareness" of what it knows and doesn't know, so that when faced with new circumstances it does not blindly assume that its prior training is going to be a fit.

Various approaches can help with this, including change detection, transfer learning, training on a diverse set of distributions, and so on. Can you guess what I am going to add to the list? You'd better be able to guess by it by now! Yes, I am suggesting that the AI Guardian Angel bot can be helpful in this aspect.

There are various ways that the AI Guardian Angel could assist the Deep AI. The obvious one involves being a mentor or safari guide to the Deep AI. You go to a safari guide to help guide you because they presumably know what to watch out for, what's safe to do, what should be avoided, etc. We have already seen this in action in our RoomboZot example.

A perhaps less obvious aspect of the interplay could be when both the Deep AI and the AI Guardian Angel bot don't know much about the environment. In this case, it is like having a second opinion for the Deep AI, somewhat informed and somewhat ill-informed. Even though the AI Guardian Angel bot might not be trained on the environment either, at least the two can confer and see what they can jointly come up with.

Suppose the RoomboZot enters into a room that it has not been in before, and likewise the AI Guardian Angel bot does not know this particular room. But, the RoomboZot has been in lots of rooms, and the AI Guardian Angel bot has monitored and aided many Deep AI cleaning robots in numerous rooms.

The Deep AI maybe opens a connection to the AI Guardian Angel bot, and asks whether it is familiar with this particular room. No, replies the AI Guardian Angel bot. Can you confer with me as I explore the room, asks the Deep AI. Yes, says the AI Guardian Angel bot. I am going to first go straight down the middle of the room, and here's my sensory data so far about the room. The AI Guardian Angel bot inspects the sensory data, and maybe it responds that for rooms like this, it has seen that it is better to zig zag rather than go straight down the middle. And so on, the collaboration continues.

OVERCOMING DEEP AI LOOPHOLES

We have covered quite a bit in this chapter. The smart robot that cleans a room has been helpful to illuminate much of what the AI Guardian Angel bot might be able to do in aiding the Deep AI when it is controlling an underlying machinery.

There was also a discussion about some popular "failure modes" of Deep AI, and besides already existing approaches to coping with those failure modes, I have tried to offer that the AI Guardian Angel bot is another potential tool for contending with those failure modes.

AI-Guardian Angel Bots: Overcoming Deep AI Loopholes

Ref	Deep AI - Problem	AI Guardian Angel Bot
1	Avoid negative side effects	Aid guidance such as indicating don't nudge the vase
2	Avoid reward hacking	Provide feedback and even tattle on Deep AI if needed
3	Have scalable oversight	Acts as 2nd opinion such as OK to clean wrappers but do not clean smart phone on the floor
4	Conduct safe explorations	Dialogues during exploration to offer insights for safety
5	Distributional shift robustness	Provides specialized "knowledge" for environments new to the Deep AI and acts as safari guide

Figure 20: Eliot – Mitigating Deep AI possible failure modes via AI-Guardian Angel Bots.

I sometimes refer to those modes as "loopholes" in what Deep AI can do. There are many approaches involved in closing those loopholes. The use of the AI Guardian Angel bot is yet another way to either close the loophole, or at least be on the look for the loopholes, and then by intention try to help the Deep AI by avoiding, detecting, or mitigating the loopholes. See Figure 20 for a quick summary of the ones we've covered in this chapter.

CHAPTER 7

MULTIPLE AGENTS: DEEP AI, AI GUARDIAN ANGEL BOTS

CHAPTER 7

MULTIPLE AGENTS: DEEP AI, AI GUARDIAN ANGEL BOTS

PREFACE

We have so far discussed the notion of a Deep AI based system that is interacting with an AI Guardian Angel bot. I refer to this as one agent interacting with one other agent. Or, in a computer-like nomenclature, let's refer to this as a 1:1 relationship.

It has been easiest to understand the underlying framework and approach by focusing on one Deep AI based system interacting with one AI Guardian Angel bot. We have used the example of a smart robot cleaning a room, wherein the RoomboZot was using Deep AI, and it conferred with an AI Guardian Angel bot that was aiding the room cleaning task.

Suppose that we had more than one Deep AI based system in that room. One such system, the RoomboZot is cleaning the room. Meanwhile, maybe the ChefboZot is a smart robot for cooking. The AI Guardian Angel bot might be conferring with both of them at the same time. Or, suppose that the RoomboZot has access to another AI Guardian Angel bot, one that also knows about room cleaning, and so the Deep AI based system opts to interact with more than one AI Guardian Angel bot. at a time We will consider these variations in this chapter.

CHAPTER 7: MULTIPLE AGENTS: DEEP AI, AI GUARDIAN ANGEL BOTS

The Deep AI based system that we have been depicting has so far been interacting with one AI Guardian Angel bot. Let's refer to this as a 1:1 relationship. We saw the two agents interacting during the example of the smart robot that was cleaning the room. This interplay will be pretty typical of what happens with a Deep AI based system that is using an AI Guardian Angel bot.

We can anticipate that the 1:1 relationship won't be the only circumstance involved in these interactions. There is the possibility that one Deep AI based system will be acting in concert with more than one AI Guardian Angel bot. Take a look at Figure 1 to see the variety of other scenarios. We will take a look at each scenario.

AI-Guardian Angel Bots: Multiple Agents Scenarios

Ref	Deep AI	AI Guardian Angel Bot
MA1	1:1	Single Deep AI interacting with single AI Guardian Angel bot, at one time and with each other
MA2	1:N Distinct	Multiple AI Guardian Angel bots interacting with same Deep AI, each bot having distinct and separate purpose or domain
MA3	1:N Overlapping	Similar to 1:N Distinct but the AI Guardian Angel bots overlap with each other and have intersecting purpose or domain
MA4	N:1	Multiple Deep AI's interacting with a single AI Guardian Angel bot, in real-time simultaneously
MA5	N:N	Multiple Deep AI's interacting with multiple AI Guardian Angel bots, many-to-many at same time

Figure 1: Eliot – Various combinations of Deep AI and AI-Guardian Angel Bots.

Figure 2 shows the 1:1 relationship. We've discussed this quite a bit. You can see that there is one Deep AI based system, and it is conferring with one AI Guardian Angel bot.

When I say conferring, I will mean that it has an open connection and the two are active in collaborating. I say this because I am trying to distinguish between a Deep AI based system that can connect with many other AI Guardian Angel bots, but it is not doing so at the moment. In other words, I might have fifty different AI Guardian Angel bots in a repository that could potentially connect with the RoomboZot smart cleaning robot. When I refer to 1:1, I mean that I am discussing what happens when one Deep AI based system confers with one AI Guardian Angel bot.

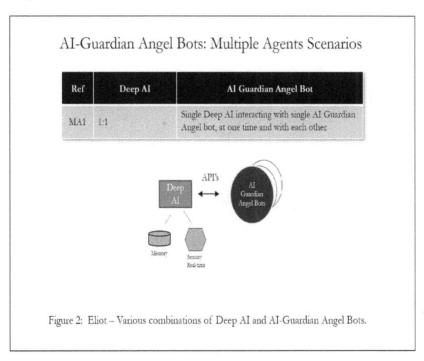

Figure 2: Eliot – Various combinations of Deep AI and AI-Guardian Angel Bots.

DEEP AI - MULTIPLE AI GUARDIAN ANGEL BOTS

Let's refer to the situation of having a 1:N relationship, meaning that we have one Deep AI based system and some number of N of the AI Guardian Angel bots, wherein N can be range from 1 to any number we might want.

There is overhead involved for the Deep AI based system to interact with these AI Guardian Angel bots, so the Deep AI based system will likely be judicious in how many AI Guardian Angel bots it will confer with at any one time.

In any case, we will explore the facets of what differences we might see when there is more than one AI Guardian Angel bot interacting with a single Deep AI system. This is important as much for the design and capabilities of the Deep AI systems as it is for the design and capabilities of the AI Guardian Angel bot.

There are two ways to consider the 1:N circumstance. First, we'll consider the circumstance of the AI Guardian Angel bots as being distinct in terms of their purpose or domain. This is what is depicted in Figure 3.

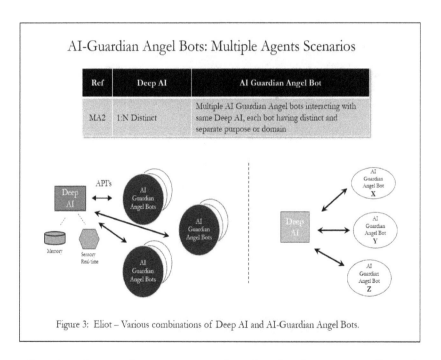

Figure 3: Eliot – Various combinations of Deep AI and AI-Guardian Angel Bots.

Imagine that we have a smart robot for cleaning a room (love that example!). We might have an AI Guardian Angel bot that is established for aiding in floor cleaning, let's call that AI Guardian Angel bot X. Let's suppose we have another AI Guardian Angel bot Y, the purpose is to aid in wall cleaning. And there is the AI Guardian Angel bot Z, which helps with cleaning of the ceiling. We will assume that the smart robot for cleaning can actually clean floors, walls, and ceilings.

It is handy then for the Deep AI based system of the smart robot to have available three AI Guardian Angel bots, each of which has a distinct specialty. Why isn't there one AI Guardian Angel bot that can help with the floor, the walls, and the ceiling? Because no one has made such a combination as yet, but put that on your To Do list.

The Deep AI based system might open a connection with all three, and do so because it is going to be cleaning the floor, the walls, and the ceiling, throughout its cleaning of the room. Rather than opening one connection to X, closing it, opening to Y, closing it, opening again with X because now it is doing the floor some more, and so on, the Deep AI based system opens a connection with each of them. This will be more efficient for the smart robot, plus, there might be something that when cleaning the floor that impacts cleaning the ceiling.

For example, suppose that in the act of cleaning the ceiling, something drips or falls onto the floor. There is then the likely need of the Deep AI based system to confer with the Z and X bots, back-and-forth, while the Deep AI is trying to figure out how to best clean the room.

Another important variation of the 1:N is the overlapping circumstance. See Figure 4.

AI-Guardian Angel Bots: Multiple Agents Scenarios

Ref	Deep AI	AI Guardian Angel Bot
MA3	1:N Overlapping	Similar to 1:N Distinct but the AI Guardian Angel bots overlap with each other and have intersecting purpose or domain

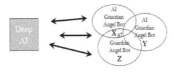

Figure 4: Eliot – Various combinations of Deep AI and AI-Guardian Angel Bots.

In Figure 4, we saw that the AI Guardian Angel bots overlap or intersect with each other. Why would this be? Suppose that the smart robot had available three AI Guardian Angel bots and each was a specialist in room cleaning. They aren't identical AI Guardian Angel bots, each is made by someone else and each has its own linage of experiences and learnings. The Deep AI based system might want to see what each of them has to say, during the room cleaning. Maybe one of the AI Guardian Angel bots knows that a vase is easily broken, but one of the other AI Guardian Angel bots does not know this. The Deep AI system can try to glean something valuable from each of the AI Guardian Angel bots.

You might be burned out now on the cleaning robot example, so let's switch over to the self-driving cars. Take a look at Figure 5.

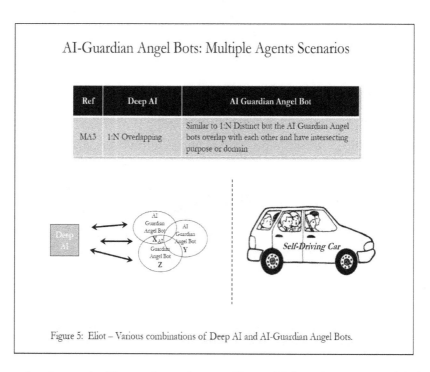

Figure 5: Eliot – Various combinations of Deep AI and AI-Guardian Angel Bots.

As shown in Figure 5, we have a Deep AI based system and it is interacting with three AI Guardian Angel bots. Let's pretend that we have a self-driving car which is equipped with Deep AI. We will then walk through an example of the interplay between the Deep AI and the three AI Guardian Angel bots that overlap.

Take a look at Figure 6. The self-driving car has people in it. Wonderful! We are going to assume that three of the passengers have AI Guardian Angel bots that they want to connect with their Deep AI of the self-driving car. Jimmy has the AI Guardian Angel bot X, Samantha has the AI Guardian Angel bot Y, and John has the AI Guardian Angel bot Z. Jimmy got his at Best Buy, Samantha bought hers on Amazon, and John pirated his off the dark web.

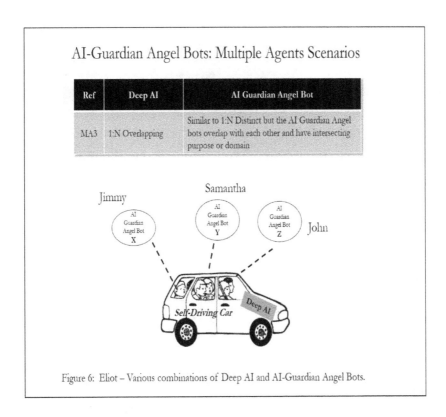

Figure 6: Eliot – Various combinations of Deep AI and AI-Guardian Angel Bots.

Why do each of them have their own AI Guardian Angel bot? Well, Jimmy is someone that prefers a very conservative way of driving. He found an AI Guardian Angel bot for self-driving cars that offers a cautious ride by conferring with the self-driving car to coach or urge the Deep AI to drive quite carefully. No need to rush and cut corners, take it easy, be as safe as possible. Samantha, in contrast, she likes a rocket experience when she is a passenger in a self-driving car. Put the pedal to the floor, and that's what her AI Guardian Angel bot is known for, indeed it is called "Radical Rocket" and has become popular among especially millennials. John is somewhat in-between the desires of Jimmy and Samantha. He has got an AI Guardian Angel bot that tries to spur a self-driving car to sometimes be conservative and sometimes be a wild driver.

Take a look at Figure 7.

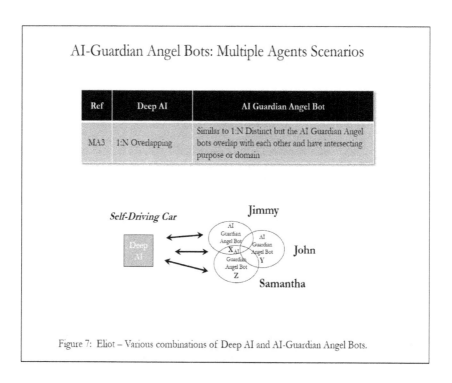

Figure 7: Eliot – Various combinations of Deep AI and AI-Guardian Angel Bots.

As you can see, I show that the three AI Guardian Angel bots overlap. How do they overlap? They all have the same overall purpose or domain, namely they provide monitoring and guidance to self-driving cars. They each have their own approach to this.

They are all using the same API's to communicate with the Deep AI system, but they have different "experiences" and approaches to what they want the Deep AI to do when operating the self-driving car.

This is different than my 1:N Distinct classification. If one of the AI Guardian Angel bots was about self-driving trucks, the other one about self-driving boats, and the other about self-driving cars, the odds are that they would rarely be used in an overlapping way. Though, I am looking forward to my self-driving car/boat/truck that I think Tesla will be delivering about the same time SpaceX gets to Mars.

Next, let's consider Figure 8. You can see that we have the AI Guardian Angel bots of X, Y, and Z. The three passengers are in the same car. They would want to have their respective AI Guardian Angel bots conferring with the self-driving car.

This might happen rather seamlessly. They carry around the bots on their smartphones, and each automatically tries to connect with whatever self-driving car they get into. Uber, Tesla, Ford, Apple's car (yes!), or whomever. If the AI Guardian Angel bot cannot make a connection to a self-driving car, it alerts the smartphone user. And, for some lesser known models of self-driving cars, the user can be prompted by some of the AI Guardian Angel bots to download an expansion pack that covers those less popular self-driving cars, just for an additional $19.99 charge.

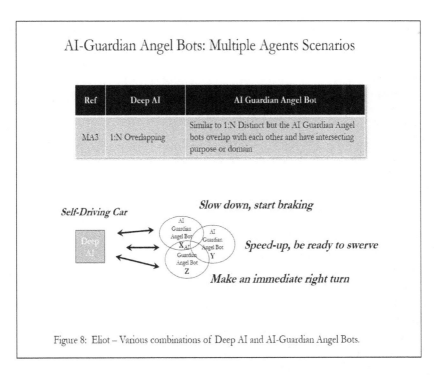

Figure 8: Eliot – Various combinations of Deep AI and AI-Guardian Angel Bots.

On this notion of overlapping, the Deep AI systems is going to need to have some means of contending with the overlapping monitoring and guidance being offered. As you can see in Figure 8, the X bot is urging the self-driving car to slow down and start braking, meanwhile the Y bot is urging to speed-up and be ready to swerve, while the Z bot is trying to get the self-driving car to make an immediate right turn.

Each of the AI Guardian Angel bots has been requesting and receiving Observations from the Deep AI systems of the self-driving car. They each have been making Predictions. Their predictions are not necessarily the same. But, let's suppose at this moment in time, they all three have ascertained that the self-driving car is reaching a point that requires a special action by the self-driving car. So, let's pretend right now that indeed all three have made a Prediction that the self-driving car needs to take some kind of action to avoid a pending crash or collision.

That being the case, their Recommendations differ. The more aggressive AI Guardian Angel bot wants the self-driving car to power its way out of the predicament. The conservative AI Guardian Angel bot wants the self-driving car to slow down and be cautious. The other AI Guardian Angel bot offers a different recommendation, wanting an immediate right turn.

What should the Deep AI do? It cannot do all three at the same time. It must choose among them. Or, it can choose none of them, and have its own Recommendation of what to do. It can negotiate with the three, trying to see what they offer as alternatives or what they each assess of other alternatives. The Deep AI is likely under time constraints to decide, since the car is barreling ahead and a choice needs to be made and acted upon.

As we will see in the next chapter, the Deep AI might opt to provide more weight to one of the AI Guardian Angel bots than the other. This might be due to "beliefs" that the Deep AI has about each of the AI Guardian Angel bot that it is interacting with.

Overall, the Deep AI will need to have some means of contending with the 1:N Overlapping class of multiple AI Guardian Angel bots. There are various ways that the Deep AI can try to assess each, and ascertain what to do. We won't cover those here and it will be a chapter in my next advanced book to get into these details.

I realize you might be in suspense about the status of Jimmy, Samantha, and Johnny in the self-driving car. What happened? Are they Okay?

You'll be glad to know that the self-driving car opted to speed-up and also make an immediate right turn. The wheels squealed, but everyone made it safely. The thing that you might note remarkably is that Jimmy, Samantha, and Johnny didn't even know that their respective AI Guardian Angel bots were protecting them and trying to get the self-driving car to take various actions. This was just assumed by them, since that was the purpose of the AI Guardian Angel bots. Working silently in the background, trying to protect each of them, in its way, on their behalf. Their guardian angels, as it were.

THE CASE OF THE N:1 AND THE N:M

We will end this chapter by considering the other multi-agent scenarios that were mentioned in Figure 1 at the start of this chapter.

Another scenario is the N:1, namely that we might have multiple Deep AI systems that are interacting in real-time with a single AI Guardian Angel bot. We'll switch back to the cleaning robot for this, but it applies in all sorts of circumstances. Our house has the ChefboZot for smart cooking by a robot, and the RoomboZot for smart cleaning by a robot. These are both Deep AI based systems. Each with its own purpose, etc.

We have an AI Guardian Angel bot in our house that serves as our house butler. It helps with a variety of aspects of managing the house. The two Deep AI based systems connect with the one AI Guardian Angel bot. Let's suppose the AI Guardian Angel bot "knows" that dinner is supposed to be served by 6:00 p.m. Meanwhile, the dining room needs to be cleaned before the guests arrive at 5:45 p.m. Plus, the ChefboZot tends to make a mess when it cooks, leaving food scraps on the floor, and at times the scraps end-up on the floor of the dining room when delivering the meal to the dining table.

The two Deep AI systems might otherwise not have any means of interplay directly between them. They are each designed and built for a specific purpose. Here, the AI Guardian Angel bot is able to communicate with both of them, and provide various guidance to each, as it also simultaneously is keeping track of both. The AI Guardian Angel bot gets the RoomboZot ready to clean the floor in the dining room, and meanwhile is gauging the timing of the completion of the cooking by the ChefboZot. And so on.

That's the N:1 scenario. The N:M scenario is that notion that we might have a multiple number of Deep AI systems that are interacting in real-time with a multiple number of AI Guardian Angel bots. This is a complex scenario.

But, it will also ultimately be a typical scenario. Once the AI Guardian Angel bots become pervasive, we can readily anticipate that there will be lots of them, and lots of Deep AI systems, and they will be interacting with each other. Welcome to the true Internet of Things (IoT), or some call it the Internet of Everything (IoE). I will be covering these complex scenarios in my advanced book.

CHAPTER 8

BELIEF SYSTEMS OF DEEP AI AND AI GUARDIAN ANGEL BOTS

CHAPTER 8

BELIEF SYSTEMS OF DEEP AI AND AI GUARDIAN ANGEL BOTS

PREFACE

Belief systems are a very important to sophisticated AI systems. In this chapter, we will take a look at how belief systems come to play for Deep AI and for AI Guardian Angel bots. Consider how your beliefs play a significant role in your daily activities. You decide to take a cab ride or maybe an Uber to get to the office today. When you do so, how do your beliefs intertwine with your decision to use the car service?

You might have a belief that a car services such as a cab or Uber is quite safe. You believe that the vehicle will be in proper shape and drivable, you believe that the driver is qualified and of a sound mind to be able to drive you. There are lots of beliefs that come to play in your decision, though you might not even be aware of how crucial your beliefs are. They are often hidden assumptions about the world around you.

Someone else might have a belief that Uber is safe, but that a regular cab is unsafe or less safe. Or, they might believe that a regular cab is safer than Uber. Why do they hold such a belief? Why does it differ from your beliefs? These are important questions to ask of any automated system that is going to be acting on behalf of people.

We need to get any hidden assumptions out and on the table when considering the interplay between the Deep AI and the AI Guardian Angel bots. This will be explored in this chapter.

———

CHAPTER 8: BELIEF SYSTEMS OF DEEP AI AND AI GUARDIAN ANGEL BOTS

Do you believe that the sun will rise in the morning? Do you believe that being a passenger in a self-driving car is safe? The nature of your beliefs guide your everyday activities. Most of the time, your beliefs are hidden from your awareness and maybe even hidden from the view of others. Nonetheless, they are there and ever present.

If you carry on a discussion with someone about their religion, suddenly your beliefs are more apparent to you and likely to the other person. Likewise if you discuss politics with someone. You hate one candidate for president and you adore the other candidate. Why? Because you have beliefs about both of the candidates. Trying to carry on a dialogue with you will be easier if I also knew what your beliefs were.

In an intelligent automated systems, we also need to consider their "beliefs" about what they are doing and the world around them. I am as usual putting into quotes words that are loaded with all sorts of connotations, such as the word "beliefs" because I don't want to confuse the notion of beliefs as humans embody them with the nature of how we might embody them in AI. For the moment, just assume that whenever I refer to beliefs for AI systems, I am not saying it is exactly like human beliefs. Take a look at Figure 1.

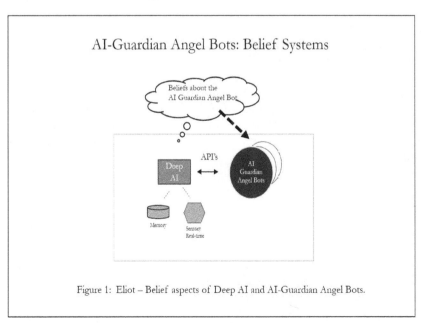

Figure 1: Eliot – Belief aspects of Deep AI and AI-Guardian Angel Bots.

As shown in Figure 1, the Deep AI system will have some kind of inner beliefs about the AI Guardian Angel bot that it is interacting with. The beliefs might be pre-programmed into the Deep AI system, such as maybe it has been coded to not trust any AI Guardian Angel systems, or maybe only trust certain ones. By trust, for the moment, consider this to mean that the Deep AI is willing to engage in a dialogue with the AI Guardian Angel bot and also willing or not willing to give consideration to what the AI Guardian Angel bot predicts, what it recommends, and also especially when it tries to do an override.

We'll use our handy robot that cleans a room for illustration of this. The RoomboZot had been cleaning the room and wanted to nudge the chair (this was discussed in a prior chapter). The AI Guardian Angel bot recommended to the Deep AI that the RoomboZot should not nudge the chair.

If the RoomboZot's Deep AI believes that the AI Guardian Angel bot is always right, then of course the Deep AI should accept the recommendation and presumably act upon it accordingly. On the other hand, if the Deep AI believes that the AI Guardian Angel bot is sometimes right but sometimes wrong, the Deep AI needs to weigh options and consider how valuable the AI Guardian Angel bots advice is. In the example, the Deep AI "decided" that the AI Guardian Angel bot was believable, but that the Deep AI judged that the concern about the nudging the chair was not overly significant, and so the Deep AI went ahead and nudged the chair.

You might also recall that the Deep AI was at a similar juncture when the vase was approached. The RoomboZot was going to nudge the vase. The AI Guardian Angel bot recommended to not nudge the vase. In this case, we also pretended that the AI Guardian Angel bot even overrode the Deep AI. This could be seen as an instance where the belief by the AI Guardian Angel bot about the dangers of nudging the vase were so strong that it outweighed the belief of the Deep AI that nudging the vase was acceptable.

ORIGINS OF BELIEF SYSTEMS

Where do these beliefs come from? As mentioned above, one manner of having beliefs might be that they have been programmed directly into the system itself. Programmers that designed and coded the Deep AI system might have placed beliefs into it, whether they know that they did or not. In essence, the developers might have carried over beliefs into the system by how they designed and coded it, doing so without the explicit realization that they were doing so. A software engineer that does not believe in AI Guardian Angel bots might decide to place into their Deep AI system that it should not trust any AI Guardian Angel bot and reject any attempts to connect to the Deep AI. This becomes an inherent belief then of the Deep AI system, as implanted by its maker.

The developer might explicitly code a belief. For example, during the design of a Deep AI system, suppose a design specification was that all recommendations from an AI Guardian Angel bot should be given due consideration, but that any overrides should be nearly always rejected. The developer would presumably dutifully establish the Deep AI to act in that manner.

There is also the aspect of belief systems that are learned over time. The Deep AI interacts with an AI Guardian Angel bot, perhaps it is the RoomboZot and the AI Guardian Angel bot that are jointly collaborating about the room cleaning. After having cleaned the room, the RoomboZot "learns" that the AI Guardian Angel bot has some handy insights, such as the aspect to not nudge the vase. If the Deep AI was somehow rewarded for not having nudged the vase (in this case, rewarded for the avoidance of an adverse side effect), it might also give due credit to the AI Guardian Angel bot. The next time that the RoomboZot cleans the room, it might opt to give the AI Guardian Angel bot even more believability and tend to lean on it more so than upon their first encounter.

Some important aspects then about belief systems then are that:

o   They can be coded into a system by its developers

o   The developers might be doing so explicitly

o   The developers might be doing so and be unawares

o   The system itself might form beliefs

o   The beliefs of the system might change over time

o   Beliefs can be learned, which offers both promise and danger

o   The beliefs tend to be hidden from view

o   The beliefs tend to guide actions

o   Beliefs about others is important in multi-agent efforts

o   The belief of one agent about the other agent must be considered

o   The beliefs of one agent about another might change over time

BELIEFS OF THE AI GUARDIAN ANGEL BOT

I focused just now on the beliefs of the Deep AI about the AI Guardian Angel bot. Well, the shoe goes on the other foot too. The AI Guardian Angel bot is going to have beliefs about the Deep AI. Once again, the beliefs might have been pre-programmed, they might be learned, etc.

Take a look at Figure 2. We might have a circumstance wherein the AI Guardian Angel bot believes that the Deep AI is not very good at what it does. Suppose that the AI Guardian Angel bot interacting with the RoomboZot believes that the Deep AI on-board is lousy. Accordingly, when interacting with the RoomboZot, the AI Guardian Angel bot is assuming that predictions and recommendations being given to the Deep AI are probably not going to be acted upon. Therefore, perhaps the AI Guardian Angel bot needs to be more insistent.

Indeed, when the RoomboZot was willing to potentially break the $18 million dollar vase, perhaps the AI Guardian Angel bot adjusted its beliefs about the Deep AI that the Deep AI is even lousier than might at first have been thought. So, the AI Guardian Angel bot is watching the behavior of the Deep AI, and if developed to do so the AI Guardian Angel bot might learn over time about the veracity of the Deep AI system.

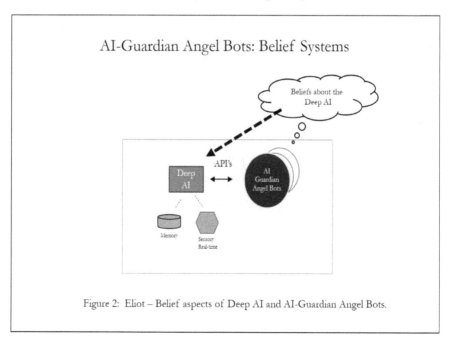

Figure 2: Eliot – Belief aspects of Deep AI and AI-Guardian Angel Bots.

In our everyday world, we are surrounded by other people's belief systems. Each time you come in contact with another human, their beliefs are sitting there inside their heads, as yours is inside your head (we might debate whether it is in our hearts too, but I think we'll accept the notion that the cognitive aspects of the brain are where beliefs reside; and don't want to get into a protracted debate about the heart/mind issue herein).

As humans, we cannot directly witness the other person's beliefs per se. Could we run an MRI to scan your brain and then inspect your beliefs? Not yet, not really. Maybe someday. So instead, we need to gauge your beliefs by secondary aspects, such as what you say, how you act, etc.

I bring up this topic because I am taking you toward the notion of Transparency. See Figure 3.

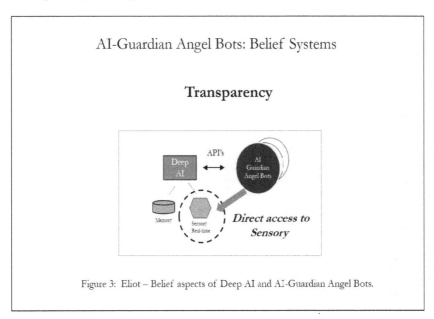

Figure 3: Eliot – Belief aspects of Deep AI and AI-Guardian Angel Bots.

Unlike humans, it is possible that one automation could directly access the beliefs of another automation. We have so far assumed that the AI Guardian Angel bot and the Deep AI were communicating via the API's that I had laid out. In that sense, they are like two humans that communicate outside of their bodies, i.e., there is no direct brain-to-brain connection. But, of course, with automation we can actually get inside the "brain" and allow direct access by either agent. This is worthwhile giving some consideration about.

TRANSPARENCY OF MULTI-AGENTS

The AI Guardian Angel bot could potentially have direct access to the sensors being used by the Deep AI system. So far, we have assumed that the AI Guardian Angel bot did not have direct access to the sensors, and instead had to request observational data based on the sensors and do so via the API's earlier defined.

You might ask, well, Lance, what difference does it make if the AI Guardian Angel bot has direct access to the sensors versus indirect access by the Deep AI relaying over data coming from the sensors? Isn't it in the end the same? Maybe not.

The Deep AI system might be obtaining the sensors data and then transforming it in some fashion. Let's pretend that the RoomboZot receives from its camera an image of an object in the room. The Deep AI tries to ascertain what the object is. It settles on the aspect that the object is a box. When the AI Guardian Angel asks for observational data from the Deep AI, what does the Deep AI provide to the AI Guardian Angel bot? Maybe it provides a transformed image taken by the camera and the transformation has filled in aspects of the image to make it appear more so like a box than does the raw image.

The AI Guardian Angel bot then receives the observational data and it also then goes along with the assumption that the object is a box. Suppose though instead that the Deep AI had provided the true raw data. Maybe the AI Guardian Angel bot upon analyzing the image data determines it is a trunk, one of those that sits in a living room and doubles as a coffee table. This might be quite important in the tasks of the Deep AI in that room. The Deep AI has not well analyzed the image, and the AI Guardian Angel bot maybe has a more powerful image analyzer or maybe knows more about the room than the Deep AI, and so can interpret the sensory data in a more enlightened way.

We therefore might consider the possibility of having the AI Guardian Angel bot reach directly to the sensors underlying the machinery that the Deep AI is controlling. If this were a self-driving car, we might have the AI Guardian Angel bot be accessing directly the sensor devices on the car such as the radar, camera, and so on. This might be in lieu of getting the data "second hand" from the Deep AI system.

Besides the interpretation and transformation problem of getting the data second-hand, there is also a cost factor of the Deep AI having to continually shovel sensory data over to the AI Guardian Angel bot, rather than allowing direct access.

On the other hand, the AI Guardian Angel bot needs to be more developed to presumably handle the sensor access. There might be a tremendous amount of software effort involved in dealing with the sensors. The AI Guardian Angel bot, if having to have all of that capability, suddenly becomes a huge system to do so.

There are all sorts of considerations about providing direct access to the sensors versus indirect via the API's. It is not an easy answer. There are some circumstances wherein direct access is warranted, and others where it probably is a worse way to go. I am not going to cover all of the advantages and disadvantages here, but just want you to know that it is not a "one shoe fits all sizes" kind of answer.

Another form of transparency is shown in Figure 4.

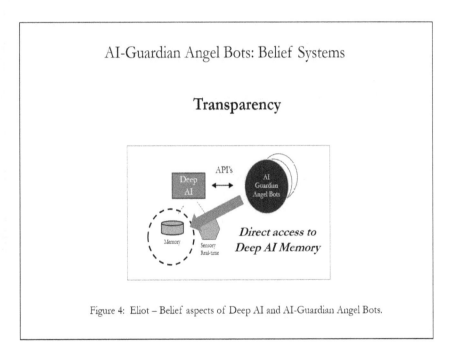

Figure 4: Eliot – Belief aspects of Deep AI and AI-Guardian Angel Bots.

We might consider giving the AI Guardian Angel bot direct access into the memory of the Deep AI system. This again might expedite the sharing of the Deep AI and the AI Guardian Angel bot. It might allow for the AI Guardian Angel bot to better gauge the beliefs of the Deep AI, including the beliefs about the AI Guardian Angel bot. If there are artificial neural networks involved in the Deep AI, which we will assume is quite likely, the question then arises as to how much good does it do the AI

Guardian Angel bot to have direct access to that? Would the AI Guardian Angel bot be able to interpret the structure, connections, weights, etc.? And, what about the processing aspects, assuming that the processing is itself not encoded into the structure.

Once again, there are advantages and disadvantages to considering whether or not to allow such direct access. The key to think about is the realization that it is a possibility. We would not readily have a similar possibility with human-to-human interaction. There is not yet a means to allow for a direct link between my brain and your brain. Sure, I am writing words on a page, you read the words on the page, and in some manner there is a transfer of my cognition to you, but it is still indirect. It is akin to the sensory data passed over to the AI Guardian Angel bot, rather than having direct access.

ASSUME NO TRANSPARENCY (OPAQUE)

For the moment, we are going to proceed with the approach that there is no direct transparency between the Deep AI and the AI Guardian Angel bots. In a sense, they are opaque to each other. See Figure 5. Therefore, they each need to consider their beliefs about the other, and combine that with whatever the other says (communicates to them) and does (acts upon). The transparency approach will be in my advanced book on this subject.

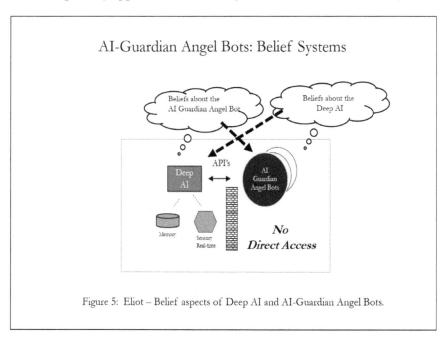

Figure 5: Eliot – Belief aspects of Deep AI and AI-Guardian Angel Bots.

BELIEFS AND THE OBSERVATIONS

Recall that we have just discussed that the observations data that the Deep AI provides to the AI Guardian Angel bot might be "suspect" in that it is maybe tainted by transformations. The transformations might be handy to the AI Guardian Angel bot in that the Deep AI has done some heavy lifting about the raw and often torrent of sensory data. When I say tainted, I don't necessarily mean that it is bad, only that the AI Guardian Angel bot needs to be established to realize that there is a layer of interpretation or transformation by the Deep AI.

In that perspective, the AI Guardian Angel bot is seeing the world through the eyes of the Deep AI system, rather than with its own eyes, as it were.

Another problem with this secondary observations is that the data will likely be a subset of the full set of data. This might have cut out some important aspects that the AI Guardian Angel bot would want to know or could use to the advantage too of the Deep AI. Figure 6 below illustrates this concept that the observational data of the Deep AI might be large, while what the AI Guardian Angel bot is getting might be much smaller.

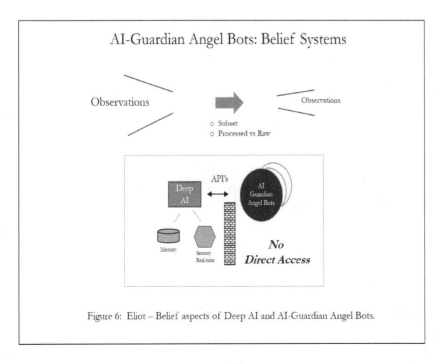

Figure 6: Eliot – Belief aspects of Deep AI and AI-Guardian Angel Bots.

And, we need to consider the element of time. The odds are that anything the Deep AI is doing will involve time. The RoomboZot cleaning the room does so over time. It is not instantaneous.

Let's use the cleaning of the room as an example. The RoomboZot does a scan with its sensors, while it is sitting still and has not yet begun its cleaning of the room. The AI Guardian Angel bot requests the observations. The Deep AI replies with the sensory data, transformed, about what it now has so far detected about the room layout and objects in the room. Suppose that the room is quiet and nothing seems to be moving.

The RoomboZot starts to clean the room. It's motion awakens a sleeping dog, which otherwise had not been detected upon the initial scan of the room. The dog charges toward the RoomboZot.

What does the AI Guardian Angel bot currently know about the room? So far, it has the initial indication of data that suggested the room was quiet. No dog, no movement. It is conceivable that by the time the AI Guardian Angel bot makes a request for more observational data, and during which let's assume it would realize too that a dog is present and in motion, meanwhile by then the dog has already chewed on the RoomboZot. Take a look at Figure 7.

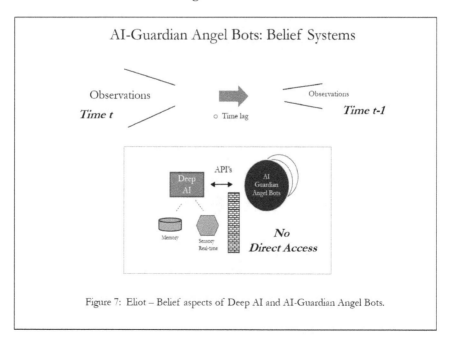

Figure 7: Eliot – Belief aspects of Deep AI and AI-Guardian Angel Bots.

There is likely to be a time lag between what the Deep AI knows and what the AI Guardian Angel bot knows. I am suggesting that when the Deep AI is at the present time of "t" we must then realize that the AI Guardian Angel bot is going to be at some prior time of "t-1" (for whatever that time lag might be, which could be milliseconds, seconds, minutes, or any length of time, depending upon what is going on regarding the communications medium and frequency of the two agents).

Take a look at Figure 8.

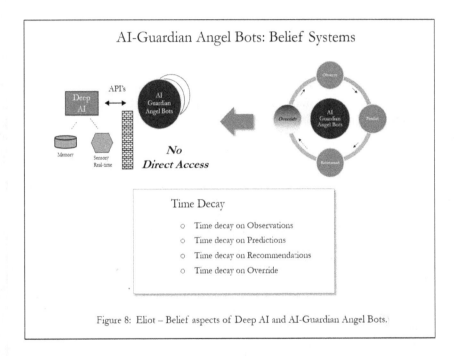

Figure 8: Eliot – Belief aspects of Deep AI and AI-Guardian Angel Bots.

This matters quite a bit, in case you were wondering why you should care. There is going to be a time lag between the two agents. We can also assume that there is a time decay factor. The observations I received just now are decaying right away as to what they really say about the environment and situation. This is also true of a prediction, it will be a prediction which had its validity at the time of the prediction being made, but might well decay rapidly thereafter.

I see my young son reaching to grab a cup full of water (I am observing). I realize that he is going to spill the cup (that's my prediction). I invoke my vocal cords and speak aloud "Don't grab the cup!" (my recommendation), but meanwhile he has already grasped the cup and the water is spilling. The time lag became a significant factor. Even my recommendation now has little value at the moment, since he has already grabbed the cup.

Worse still, supposing upon then hearing my words, my son decides that since I urged him to not grab the cup, he will go ahead and drop the cup. The spill gets even worse! My recommendation suffered a time decay and yet the receiver of the recommendation did not realize that my recommendation was really just for a particular moment in time for a particular set of circumstances.

TIME FACTOR

Thus, taking into account the factor of time will be an essential aspect to the Deep AI and AI Guardian Angel bot interplay. They will have beliefs about each other, and be communicating with each other, but those communications and those beliefs are changing over time, plus the environment and the situation is changing over time.

Any observational data must be time stamped and considered to be of that time. Any predictions likewise, as will be the case for any recommendations and overrides. The Deep AI and AI Guardian Angel bot live in a world that is run by time. Time must be taken into consideration.

I say this because those that aren't used to developing systems that interact in real-time are less familiar with the importance of time in the design and constructs of the system. I am not suggesting that time as a factor is unique to the Deep AI and AI Guardian Angel bots. If you are developing a systems for a Point-of-Sale (POS) device in a grocery store, you need to consider time. The consumer swipes their credit card, the POS provides the credit card info, the system checks to see if the credit card is valid. Time is of the essence. Suppose the consumer swipes the card a second time, thinking that the POS did not get the first swipe. The grocery store system now gets two swipes of the same card. Is it one charge or maybe is it two different charges?

The Deep AI when receiving anything from the AI Guardian Angel bot needs to assess the timing of what it received. Similarly, the AI Guardian Angel bot needs to consider the same about anything it gets from the Deep AI. The AI Guardian Angel bot, if being the main requestor, must also anticipate a time delay between when requested and when receiving a reply. There is a vital dance between the Deep AI and the AI Guardian Angel bot that makes time integral to their collaboration.

DON'T HAVE

In a perfect world, whatever the AI Guardian Angel bot asks of the Deep AI will return an answer. Similarly, if the Deep AI asks the Angel bot for something, the AI Guardian Angel bot will provide an answer. In a laboratory this might be feasible, but in a real-world setting the circumstances might not provide an "answer" in the sense that we are considering the word.

See Figure 9.

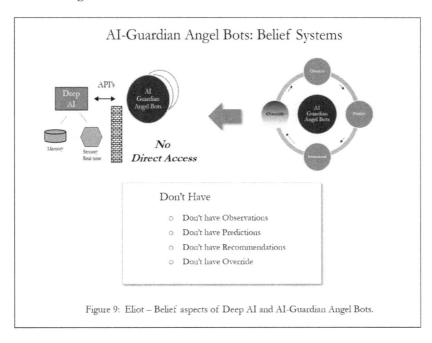

Figure 9: Eliot – Belief aspects of Deep AI and AI-Guardian Angel Bots.

The agent might not have what the other is asking for. Suppose the RoomboZot is considering whether to nudge the vase. The Deep AI decides to get a second opinion. It sends a request to the AI Guardian Angel bot, seeking its latest prediction regarding the vase. The AI Guardian Angel bot maybe has not yet arrived at a prediction. It is taking time to figure things out, or maybe it lacks sufficient observational data to make a prediction. Either way, sometimes the agent will tell the other it doesn't know. The other agent needs to then decide what to do about this.

If given a "Don't Know" the other agent might decide that if time proceeds that then the other agent might know, giving it time to ascertain say a recommendation. Or, maybe the other agent needs to supply more observation data and then the other agent will be in a better posture to provide an answer.

We can at least though say that a "Don't Know" is an actual answer. I compare this to no answer at all, i.e., silence. If I don't respond to you, that's harder to say it is an answer, since it could be that I've fallen asleep or that I've left the room. We can quibble over this, but the point is that at least a "Don't Know" is a definite response, and it does convey to the other agent something about what the respondent knows and doesn't know. This must be taken into consideration by both the Deep AI and the AI Guardian Angel bots.

DISPUTES

The Deep AI and the AI Guardian Angel bots will dispute each other. See Figure 10.

The RoomboZot disputed the prediction and recommendation of the AI Guardian Angel bot about the aspect of nudging the chair. The Deep AI thought it was okay to do, while the AI Guardian Angel bot expressed that it should not do so.

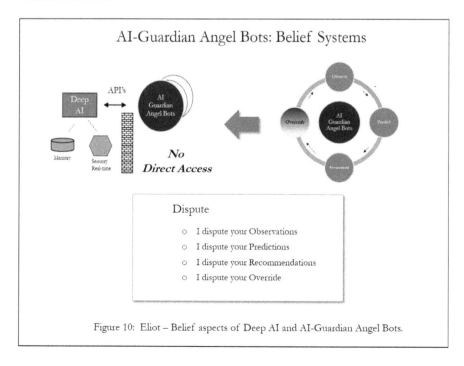

Figure 10: Eliot – Belief aspects of Deep AI and AI-Guardian Angel Bots.

The two agents need to be able to communicate with each other about disputes. It is important in their collaboration. They are not always going to agree. One might say that the keenest value is when a dispute arises, because it suggests that one of them has differing assumptions or awareness than the other, and if they confer it might be helpful to both parties. The self-driving car might not have ascertained that speeding up the car would avoid a collision, and instead be indicating it is going to slow down. The AI Guardian Angel bot suggesting to speed-up could jar the Deep AI into considering another option. This could be due to dispute between them.

CORROBORATE

If we are going to allow for disputes, we should also be allowing for corroboration. You might think that if the two agents agree, there is no need to formally acknowledge it.

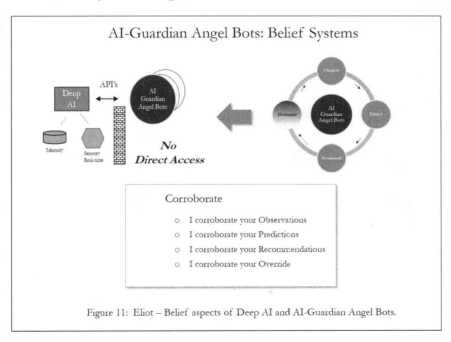

Figure 11: Eliot – Belief aspects of Deep AI and AI-Guardian Angel Bots.

Suppose for example that the Deep AI wants sweep up the candy wrappers, and the AI Guardian Angel bot has reached that same recommendation, but it does not convey as such to the Deep AI that it also reached that same recommendation. Would silence on the part of the AI

Guardian Angel bot imply that it agrees? Well, we are in some murky turf if we begin to play the game that silence means agreement. Again, the connection might be severed. It might be that the AI Guardian Angel bot is still calculating its recommendation, and so on.

It is better to have each corroborate with the other when they are in agreement. This also helps for learning purposes. I know more about you, and you know more about me, by us each considering how many times and in what ways we have corroborated each other.

CERTAINTY

Another facet of multi-agent interaction involves Certainty. The interaction between two automations normally assumes that each is fully certain about whatever they convey to each other. The POS device is "certain" of the credit card info that it hands over to the grocery store main system. The grocery store main system is "certain" when it responds to grant the transaction. There is often no provision for uncertainty in these system to system interactions.

See Figure 12, regarding the certainty aspects here.

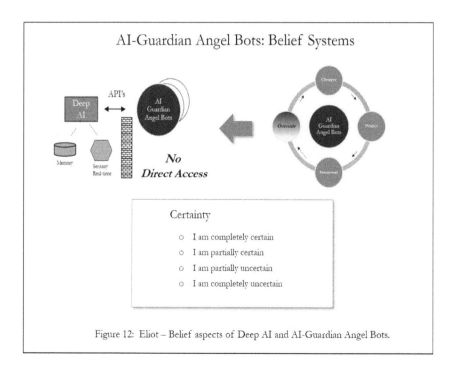

Figure 12: Eliot – Belief aspects of Deep AI and AI-Guardian Angel Bots.

When the RoomboZot received a prediction from the AI Guardian Angel bot that the nudging of the chair might harm the chair, the AI Guardian Angel bot attached an indication of certainty associated with the prediction. The AI Guardian Angel bot indicated it was only partially certain about the outcome. The Deep AI of the RoomboZot had made its own prediction, which was that nudging the chair would not harm the chair. The Deep AI attached a certainty that it was completely certain of this prediction.

This then led the Deep AI to consider its own prediction, which was nudging the chair is okay and with a very high certainty, versus the second opinion offered by the AI Guardian Angel bot that nudging the chair might be harmful but that it was only partially certain about this. Based on its own certainty and based on the lesser certainty of the AI Guardian Angel bot, the Deep AI opted to proceed with the nudging of the chair.

Most of what the AI Guardian Angel bot and the Deep AI are going to be doing will involve varying levels of certainty attached to it. Predictions will have various levels of certainty. Recommendations will have varying levels, and so will Overrides. This is another important aspect of how the two systems will interact.

Each provides its certainly level to the other, doing so as warranted during their dialogue. Circumstances are changing over time, as previously noted. Therefore, the certainty of a prediction at moment in time t, might increase at time t+1, or might decrease. Certainty is a belief.

For example, I look at my son as he reaches to grab a cup full of water, and I am "certain" that his grabbing the cup will spill the water. What is my level of certainty in this case? Let's say that I think I am 100% certain of it. He grabs the cup, and it turns out that the water does not spill, maybe because it is a spill proof cup. At the time before he grabbed the cup, I was 100% it would spill, and now I am no longer so certain. Your belief about another person will be partially based on their ability to gauge certainty levels and be good or bad at the certainty that they attach.

If a Deep AI system is interacting with an AI Guardian Angel bot that is never certain about anything, the Deep AI might be hesitant to abide by its recommendations. If the AI Guardian Angel bot is very certain and it turns out that it is correct much of the time, the Deep AI might "learn" to more readily trust the AI Guardian Angel bot and thusly adopt its recommendations.

OBSERVATIONS ACCURACY

The observations data that is being provided to the AI Guardian Angel bot will vary in terms of whether it is considered accurate or not. Why wouldn't it be perfectly accurate? Suppose the camera sensor is acting up and has a hardware malfunction, and so it is providing partially goofed-up data. Or, maybe the dog slobbered on the RoomboZot's camera and so now all images are blurry.

When providing the observations data to the AI Guardian Angel bot, it will be helpful for the Deep AI system to attach a sense of accuracy to the data being conveyed. The granularity of the accuracy will depend upon the sensors and the aspects of those sensors.

Take a look at Figure 13. As shown, the Deep AI system might believe the data to be accurate, or it might believe the data to be inaccurate. For inaccurate data, the belief might that in spite of the inaccuracies it is nonetheless still acceptable for use, or that it is unacceptable. The Deep AI might also have no belief about the accuracy of the data.

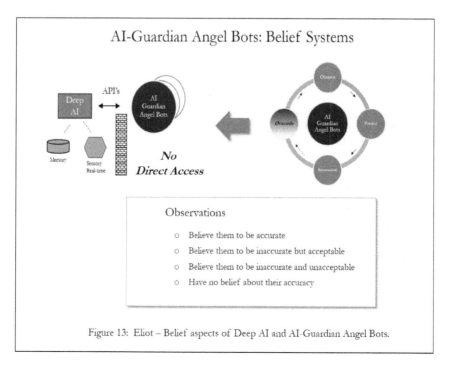

Figure 13: Eliot – Belief aspects of Deep AI and AI-Guardian Angel Bots.

The AI Guardian Angel bot needs to consider the accuracy beliefs of the Deep AI system. If the Deep AI believes that the observations are accurate, then presumably they can be relied upon. On the other hand, if the Deep AI is labeling it as inaccurate and unacceptable, the AI Guardian Angel bot will need to take this into account when making predictions and recommendations. It is bound to impact the certainty that the AI Guardian Angel bot will attach to the predictions and recommendations.

BELIVING IN EACH OTHER

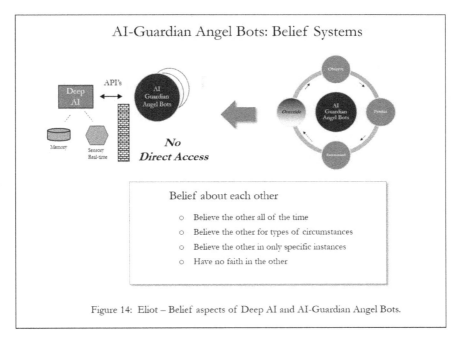

Figure 14: Eliot – Belief aspects of Deep AI and AI-Guardian Angel Bots.

Take a look at Figure 14. There are aspects of the two agents in terms of believing in each other. By believing in each other I suggest that they are willing to engage in a dialogue with the other and genuinely consider the merits of the dialogue. If they entirely disbelieve each other, it is unlikely to be a very productive dialogue. Each will disregard what the other has to say.

The Deep AI might believe fully in the AI Guardian Angel bot all of the time. This is probably the case when they have already had an established relationship, or have been programmed to accept this fate. For much of the time, the two agents will believe in each other to varying degrees over the course of their interaction and as based on certain types of circumstances. The RoomboZot might be more believing in the AI Guardian Angel bot for its advice when in a room that is a dining room, but less so when in a kitchen. Or, maybe the AI Guardian Angel bot knows a lot about vases and the Deep AI believes that whenever a vase arises, the use of the AI Guardian Angel bot is especially handy.

AGREEMENT/DISAGREEMENT

Previously, we saw that the two agents will have disputes, and they will corroborate, when the occasions are relevant and warranted to do so. In Figure 15, we add the belief of agreement and disagreement with each other, which is related to the disputing and corroborating aspects mentioned earlier.

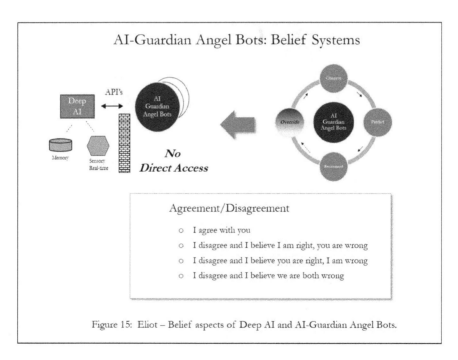

Figure 15: Eliot – Belief aspects of Deep AI and AI-Guardian Angel Bots.

As shown, the Deep AI might indicate to the AI Guardian Angel bot that it agrees with something that the AI Guardian Angel bot has indicated, such as a recommendation. Or, it might disagree with the AI Guardian Angel bot. The disagreement might also cause the Deep AI to believe that the AI Guardian Angel bot is wrong. The disagreement could cause the

Deep AI to decide it is wrong itself and that the AI Guardian Angel bot is right.

There is also the possibility that the Deep AI realizes that it is wrong and the AI Guardian Angel is also wrong. Does this mean that indeed both of them are wrong? Not necessarily. Remember this is a belief. The belief and the real-world are often different from each other. I see a person holding a sign that says the world will end tomorrow. I disagree. Furthermore, I think the person is wrong. Meanwhile, I believe the world will end on my birthday next year. Let's assume (for all our sakes), I am also wrong. We are both wrong about our beliefs of the world. This can happen.

LEARNING SOMETHING

The last belief aspect that we'll cover in this chapter is about the belief in learning. See Figure 16.

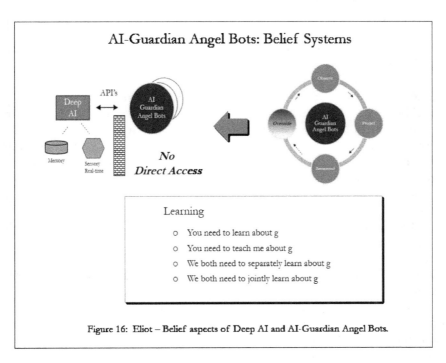

Figure 16: Eliot – Belief aspects of Deep AI and AI-Guardian Angel Bots.

As a former Computer Science professor, I would often urge a student to learn about something, like learn about the Big-O complexity of algorithms. I did so because I hoped it would help them in their quest to become a good computer scientist.

For sophisticated Deep AI and AI Guardian Angel bots, it could be that the Deep AI indicates to the AI Guardian Angel bot that it should learn about the aspect of pets when cleaning a room. Let's assume that the RoomboZot already knows somewhat about this topic. Let's assume that the AI Guardian Angel bot does not. It could be that the Deep AI has detected that the AI Guardian Angel bot is clueless about pets, and in order to carry on a dialogue in a room that has pets, it is advising the AI Guardian Angel bot to learn about pets.

How would the AI Guardian Angel bot learn about pets? Suppose there is a "pet expansion pack" associated with the AI Guardian Angel bot, and so it is able to download it from a repository and now it "knows" about pets in a cleaning of a room scenario. That's of course a pretty easy way to have learned about the topic.

A more impressive aspect would be for the AI Guardian Angel bot to add into its own structure the notion of a pet, and then over time be observing pets via the RoomboZot and its Deep AI. Plus, doing likewise with other Deep AI systems that are in the house that the AI Guardian Angel bot also has access to.

We might also envision that one agent would be willing to "teach" the other agent about something. For example, suppose the AI Guardian Angel bot indicates to the Deep AI that it would be handy if the Deep AI could teach it about pets. The Deep AI might be able to transfer some of its "knowledge" about pets in a cleaning scenario over to the AI Guardian Angel bot.

As with all of these aspects, the AI Guardian Angel bot needs to be wary about what it learns. Maybe the teaching of the Deep AI about pets is good in some ways, and bad in other ways. The Deep AI has perhaps over time learned a belief that pets can be run over by the RoomboZot and do so with no harm to the pet. Should the AI Guardian Angel bot have that same belief, simply because its teacher did?

There is another sophisticated aspect that might be considered, namely the joint learning by both the Deep AI and the AI Guardian Angel bot. Into the room comes a Barbie doll that walks and talks, on its own (thanks, Mattel!). The RoomboZot Deep AI has never seen this before. The AI Guardian Angel bot has never experienced it either. Suppose they figure out it is not a pet, i.e., it is not a living creature. It is not a chair, it is not a table, etc. It is an object that moves around, makes sounds, and they've not ever seen this before. The two agents could potentially jointly learn about the Barbie doll together, sharing what they each know, believe, or can guess about this unusual thing or creature.

RECAP OF BELIEF SYSTEM

I sometimes get asked, why is Deep AI and these AI Guardian Angel bots any different than any other kind of app? I would offer that another distinction is that for these to be robust, they need to take into account their own belief system and their belief in other agents that they interact with.

See Figure 17. We have covered in this chapter some of the fundamentals involved. Each agent needs to establish and utilize what beliefs it has about its own abilities and the abilities and "judgment" of the other. They do this by providing certainty to their communications, they deal with time factors, they take into the accuracy of what they are observing, and so on.

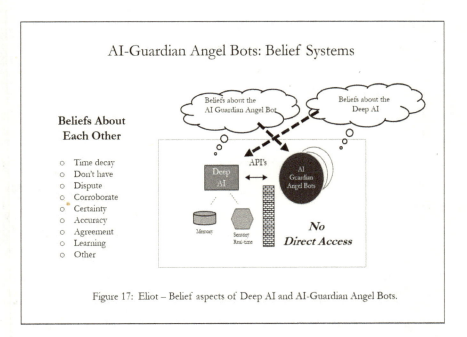

Figure 17: Eliot – Belief aspects of Deep AI and AI-Guardian Angel Bots.

BELIEF SYSTEM TRUST QUADRANT

We end this chapter with a handy four-square quadrant. Take a look at Figure 18.

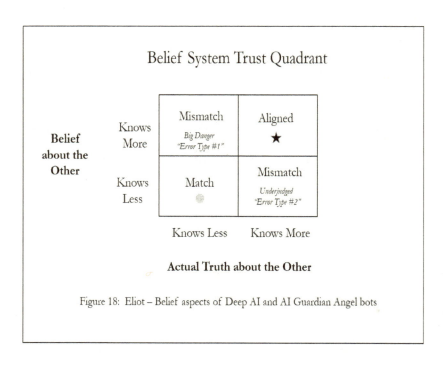

Figure 18: Eliot – Belief aspects of Deep AI and AI Guardian Angel bots

As you can see, there is a vertical axis consisting of the belief about the other. The horizontal axis has the actual truth about the other.

The context is the belief of whether the other knows more or less than what the one believes they do. Kind of confusing, let me clarify. In my interacting with another person, I am likely to judge whether they know more about a topic than I do. I met someone the other day that was an expert at fly fishing. I grant them that they know more about this topic than I do. I met someone that was taking a beginning programming class in Python. I know for sure that I know more than they do.

The belief about what the other persons knows or does not know is shapes how you interact with the other person and collaborate with them. If the person that knows fly fishing tells me that my fishing pole needs to be at least six feet long, I will likely readily adopt this advice because I believe they know more about it than me.

Let's take another look at Figure 18 (see below, shown again for ease of reference while on this page).

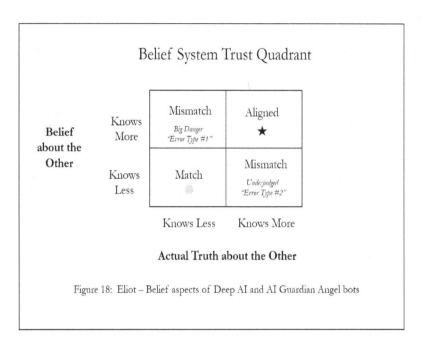

Figure 18: Eliot – Belief aspects of Deep AI and AI Guardian Angel bots

In Figure 18, you can see that the harboring of a belief about the other can be correctly assessed, such as believing that the other knows less and they really do, or that they know more and they really do. Those are relatively safe circumstances. Where we can get ourselves in trouble is when we incorrectly assess and believe that the other agent knows more and they actually know less (I call this "Big Danger"), or when we believe the other agent knows less when they really know more ("Underjudged").

The reason that the upper left quadrant, labeled as Error Type #1, can be viewed as a big danger is that if we believe the other agent knows more than we do, but they don't actually know more, we can be lulled into believing them and taking action over what we might believe ourselves. I meet a professional race car driver. The driver tells me that I can put purified water in my gas tank and it will increase my car performance and

MPG. I believe that the race car driver knows more about cars than I do, and even though it seems kind of fishy about putting water into my gas tank, well, I believe that the race car driver is probably onto something good.

Error Type #2 is not quite as bad. This is when I believe that the other agent knows less but they actually know more. I interact with the person taking the Python class and I assume they know nothing about how to handle exceptions in their code. Turns out they know a lot about it. I underjudged them. This can create difficulties such as elongating a decision making process needlessly, or alienating the other agent, etc. Generally, though, the chances of a getting sideways and into harm's way is not as pronounced as with Error Type #2.

The Deep AI will be formulating various granular beliefs about the AI Guardian Angel bot. How well will it assess the overall nature and depth of the knowledge of the AI Guardian Angel bot. It might gauge it correctly and assess well whether the AI Guardian Angel bot knows less or more than itself, or it might misjudge and get itself sideways by doing so. This is another consideration in the design, building, and evolution for both the Deep AI systems and the AI Guardian Angel bots.

CHAPTER 9

DESIGN PATTERNS FOR AI GUARIDAN ANGEL BOTS

CHAPTER 9

DESIGN PATTERNS FOR
AI GUARDIAN ANGEL BOTS

PREFACE

In this chapter, I will cover some overarching system design patterns that provide an additional indication about the AI Guardian Angel bots and their internal processing. We will begin by revisiting the four stage model that has been used through this book, and then extend it for purposes of looking more deeply into facets of the model.

For those of you not familiar with the concept of system design patterns, the notion is that when developing software it can be helpful to have various templates available. These templates, referred to as patterns, allow for other software developers to have a reusable solution that they can incorporate into their system development work. The patterns are usually generalized so that they can be readily reused for other specific circumstances.

The patterns shown here are illustrative of the AI Guardian Angel bot processing, provide a deeper sense of the processing involved, and are a stepping off point for further work by other AI Guardian Angel bot researchers, developers, and the like.

———————

CHAPTER 9: DESIGN PATTERNS FOR AI GUARDIAN ANGEL BOTS

Within computer science and systems development, there is an area of focus that involves identifying and promoting system design patterns. There are various names given to this field of endeavor, along with various flavors of design patterns, some of which are structural in nature and others more processing or behavior oriented in nature.

The overall notion is to provide a kind of pattern or template that can be reused by others. Rather than having to start a software effort or systems effort from scratch, a developer or software engineer can peruse a set of design patterns to see what they might leverage. Some of the design patterns might be utilized as is, some might be refined, and others might not be of any relevance to the matter of the particular development work at-hand.

I provide in this chapter a set of nine design patterns that are behavior oriented and are pertinent to the AI Guardian Angel bot. By behavior oriented, this means that they illustrate the processing aspects of the AI Guardian Angel bot, rather than the structural aspects.

The purpose for providing these design patterns includes:

o   Convey a sense of what kind of processing will be undertaken by an AI Guardian Angel bot,

o   Start the effort toward establishing a library of such design patterns and foster an open source approach to AI Guardian Angel bot evolution,

o   Serve as an impetus for further research on the advent of AI Guardian Angel bots and how they will work,

o   Spark efforts to develop reusable code and components for the rapid development of AI Guardian Angel bots.

EXTENDING THE FOUR STAGE MODEL

Let's start by revisiting the four stage model that was introduced earlier in this book. Take a look at Figure 1 below.

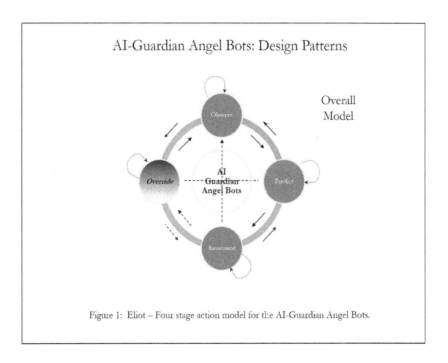

AI-Guardian Angel Bots: Design Patterns

Overall
Model

Figure 1: Eliot – Four stage action model for the AI-Guardian Angel Bots.

This is the same familiar looking four stage model, consisting of the Observe, Predict, Recommend, Override stages.

What makes this version look a bit different is the additional of several arrows. These arrows weren't shown on the earlier version to avoid making the model seem overly complex. The addition of the arrows adds a modest sense of complexity, but not really much complexity once you've had a chance to comprehend the purpose underlying the added aspects.

There are now loops on each of the four stages, such that the Observe has a loop, the Predict has a loop, the Recommend has a loop, and the Override has a loop. There are also now arrows showing a back-and-forth aspect between each nearby stage, and some across the model itself. We will explore each of these extensions next.

OBSERVATIONS-PATTERN (O-P)

The first design pattern that we'll discuss is called the Observations-pattern, or I'll use O-p as a short way to refer to it. Take a look at Figure 2.

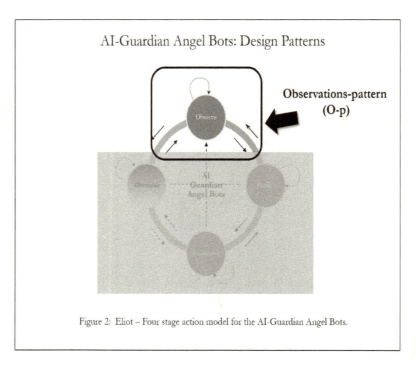

AI-Guardian Angel Bots: Design Patterns

Observations-pattern
(O-p)

Figure 2: Eliot – Four stage action model for the AI-Guardian Angel Bots.

I have placed bolded box around the part of the model that we are now discussing, and shaded the other parts so they are not visually in the way.

The Observations pattern consist of a processing of observations. Recall that when discussing the API's for the AI Guardian Angel bot, we introduced an API that involves requesting an observation from the Deep AI system of interest, and then receiving back from the Deep AI system a response to that request.

We have also covered the aspect that the AI Guardian Angel bot needs to be suspicious of the observations provided, since they might be inaccurate and/or they might be accompanied by an interpretation or transformation that was imposed by the Deep AI.

The O-p is a handy design pattern that indicates the AI Guardian Angel bot will normally be repeatedly or iteratively getting observations from the Deep AI (thus, the loop that arises from the Observe stage and comes back to the Observe stage).

Upon each request and receipt of observations from the Deep AI, the AI Guardian Angel bot will need to process those observations. This processing will include inspecting what has been provided, determining the veracity of the observations, and then analyzing the observations.

The AI Guardian Angel bot is likely to be collecting the observations and gauging them over time. Recall that we have discussed that time is a crucial aspect to nearly any circumstance of the Deep AI and AI Guardian Angel bot. How long ago were the observations collected by the Deep AI? Does the time lag between then and now present any concerns by the AI Guardian Angel bot?

There is also the question of how fast and frequently this loop should be undertaken. If the environment involved is relative stable and unchanging, and if the underlying machinery being controlled by the Deep AI is unmoving, and if there are few likely risks of something suddenly entering into the environment that would pose a safety concern, presumably the looping can then be less frequent.

Of course, the notion of fast and frequent is relative. For the RoomboZot cleaning robot, it might be sufficient to get observations every second or maybe tenth of a second. For a self-driving car, moving ahead at 70 miles per hour, the timing and frequency of the interaction might be more akin to milliseconds or even faster.

The AI Guardian Angel bot is also likely to be trying to match the observations to its own set of prior observations, both those observations being taken now and ones from history or that it was trained on. For example, how is the AI Guardian Angel bot for the robot cleaning scenario going to be able to recognize there is a vase in the room? It would analyze the observations and compare to prior indications of objects.

When the AI Guardian Angel bot was first developed, perhaps it was infused with images and other attributes of vases. Then, once in use, it might have been "learning" more about vases and have become more adept at ascertaining what is a vase. During the moment at which observations are being obtained and analyzed, the AI Guardian Angel bot might be further refining its ability to identify vases, simultaneous with trying to ascertain whether the image at hand is a vase or not.

This loop of the Observe stage will continue until a threshold has been reached that the AI Guardian Angel bot opts to enter into the next stage, the Predict stage. Do not though think of this model is strictly serial in its processing. The Observe loop can be continuing to occur, meanwhile the AI Guardian Angel bot has stepped into the next design pattern too.

OBSERVATIONS-PREDICT PATTERN (OP-P)

The next design pattern is the Observations-Predict pattern, referred to as OP-p. See Figure 3.

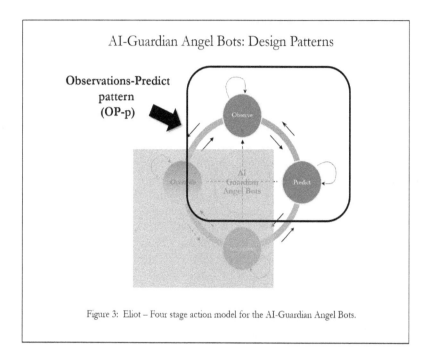

Figure 3: Eliot – Four stage action model for the AI-Guardian Angel Bots.

As shown, this design pattern consists of the Observation stage moving into the Predict stage. After reaching a point of the observations being sufficient suitable to utilize, the Predict stage examines the observations and makes predictions of what might occur next.

The predictions are both short-range and long-range, wherein range refers to both distance and time. For example, the RoomboZot might be predicted by the AI Guardian Angel bot to be headed towards the chair (short-range from it, short time from it), and be headed next to the vase (long-range from it, long time from it).

As part of the usual purpose of the AI Guardian Angel bot, the predictions are also about what issues or dangers might be arising. For example, that the long-range heading to the vase might lead to damage to the vase.

PREDICTIONS-PATTERN (P-P)

The next of the design patterns is shown in Figure 4. This is the Predictions-pattern or P-p design.

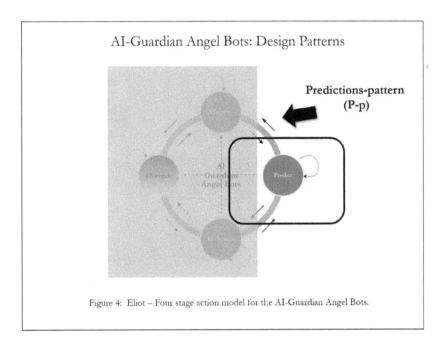

Figure 4: Eliot – Four stage action model for the AI-Guardian Angel Bots.

Similar to the Observations-pattern (O-p), this shows a tight looping of the Predict stage. The same rationale applies, namely that we would want to iteratively or repeatedly make predictions.

The number of predictions could be endless. So, the AI Guardian Angel bot needs to be evaluating what predictions are worthy of developing and which ones are not. Again, under the assumption that a key purpose of the AI Guardian Angel bot is to ensure safety and avoid harmful results of the Deep AI, it should be especially devoted to finding predictions that have such outcomes.

Predicting that the RoomboZot is going to roll along the floor is not an especially useful prediction per se. Predicting that the RoomboZot is going to collide with a pet or damage an object in the room, these are predictions worthy of identifying. Thus, there is a boundedness to the predictions looping.

PREDICT-RECOMMEND PATTERN (PR-P)

The next design pattern consists of the Predict-Recommend, labeled as PR-p, as shown in Figure 5.

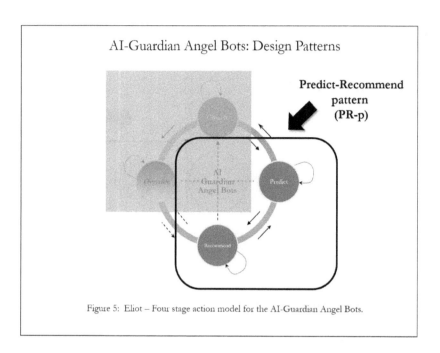

Figure 5: Eliot – Four stage action model for the AI-Guardian Angel Bots.

The Predict-Recommend pattern consists of moving from the Predict stage to the Recommend stage. Again, I want to emphasize this is not a serial approach and there is an implied parallelism going on, such that the looping of the Predict (P-p) and the looping of the Observe (O-p) can still be taking place.

Here, the nature of the predictions, by their magnitude, their chances for indicating harmful outcomes, and so on, will lead the AI Guardian Angel bot to move toward coming up with recommendations about what to do or not do.

For example, the AI Guardian Angel bot might be predicting that the self-driving car will not be able to safely make the curve up ahead on the mountain road due to going too fast, and the prediction leads to a recommendation by the AI Guardian Angel bot that the self-driving car should slow down as it heads toward the endangering curve.

RECOMMENDS PATTERN (R-P)

Next, we'll take a look at the Recommends pattern, called R-p. See Figure 6.

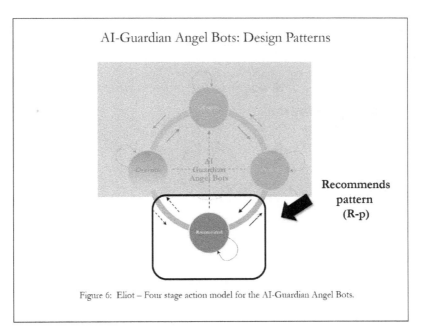

AI-Guardian Angel Bots: Design Patterns

Recommends pattern (R-p)

Figure 6: Eliot – Four stage action model for the AI-Guardian Angel Bots.

Once again, we have an iterative loop taking place. Here, the Recommend stage is deriving numerous recommendations. The recommendations are based on the predictions, which are based on the observations. The recommendations are also based on the "knowledge" of the AI Guardian Angel bot, including what kinds of recommendations have been successful in the past and whether they might be applicable in this case.

I say that because the number of recommendations is essentially boundless. The AI Guardian Angel bot could recommend that the RoomboZot not fly in the air. But, this recommendation does not make much sense in the context of the circumstance. There is no reason to believe that the RoomboZot can fly, so why produce a recommendation that it should not fly? The point being that the recommendations are bounded and purposely so by the AI Guardian Angel bot. It is intended to focus on recommendations that are pertinent to the predictions and for the safety of the tasks underway by the Deep AI.

RECOMMEND-OVERRIDE PATTERN (ROV-P)

In Figure 7, there is the Recommend-Override pattern (ROV-p). This consists of the Recommend stage going into the Override stage.

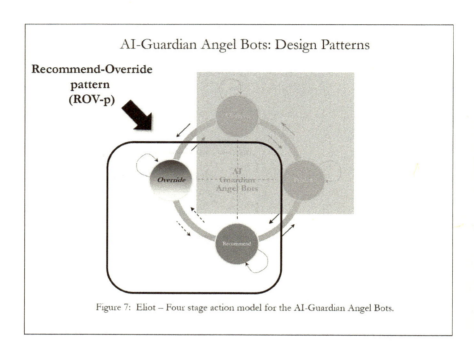

Figure 7: Eliot – Four stage action model for the AI-Guardian Angel Bots.

As a reminder, this shift into the Override stage from the Recommend stage is taking place likely in parallel with the other design patterns. In any case, the Recommend consists predominantly of recommendations for the Deep AI that involve the Deep AI avoiding any safety issues or harmful results. As such, and wanting to serve in the guardian angel manner, the AI Guardian Angel is especially interested in whether the Deep AI is going to make use of the recommendations.

If the Deep AI has opted to continue on its course of action and as such would be leading to the predicted harmful results and that it is not abiding by the recommendation of the AI Guardian Angel bot, the AI Guardian Angel bot would then attempt to override the Deep AI. This should be a last resort effort by the AI Guardian Angel bot. Most of the time, it is hoped that the Deep AI is sound enough to have avoided getting itself into this kind of situation.

OVERRIDE PATTERN (OV-P)

The next design pattern is the Override pattern, denoted as OV-p. Take a look at Figure 8.

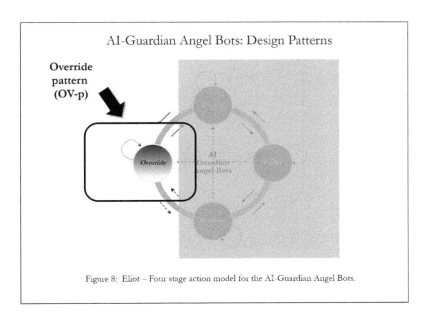

Figure 8: Eliot – Four stage action model for the AI-Guardian Angel Bots.

As indicated, and similar to the other tight iterative loops on the other three stages, this is an iterative loop on the Override stage.

Why might this occur? Suppose the AI Guardian Angel bot has determined via the predictions, as based on the observations, an upcoming harmful result, and has issued a recommendation or maybe even a series of recommendations, and then opted to attempt an override of the Deep AI because the severity and consequences are dire.

There will be differing circumstances about the ability of the AI Guardian Angel bot to override the Deep AI. If we were to allow the AI Guardian Angel bot to override whenever it pleases to do so, this could be quite disruptive to the Deep AI, and we are also assuming that most of the time the Deep AI is going to be "doing the right thing" and won't need an override.

We might have circumstances wherein the override is never allowed per se and only considered as another kind of recommendation.

OBSERVE-OVERRIDE PATTERN (OOV-P)

The next of the design patterns is the Observe-Override pattern, labeled as OOV-p. See Figure 9.

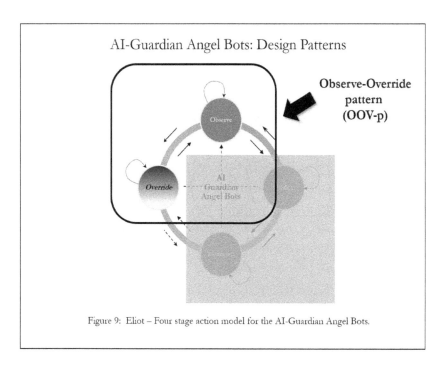

Figure 9: Eliot – Four stage action model for the AI-Guardian Angel Bots.

How will the AI Guardian Angel bot "know" whether or not the Deep AI actually undertook the override, assuming that an override was provided and enacted? One means to be aware of whether the override occurred would be for the Deep AI to tell the AI Guardian Angel bot, which is a provision of the API involved. But, telling and doing can be two different things.

So, the AI Guardian Angel bot would want get further observations, and from those, it would be able to ascertain whether the override is in-process, and whether the override was enacted. Plus, what the override might have also done within the environment and therefore what might need to be done next.

For example, a self-driving car that has slowed to meet the demands of a tight curve, might then next find itself in a consequent difficulty because a car is coming up from behind at a fast speed and might collide. The AI Guardian Angel bot needs to keep continually updating to the circumstances.

OBSERVE-PREDICT-RECOMMEND (OPR-P)

The last of the design patterns covered herein is the Observe Predict Recommend pattern, shown in Figure 9. It is the first of these patterns that involves more than two of the stages. The pattern is labeled as OPR-p.

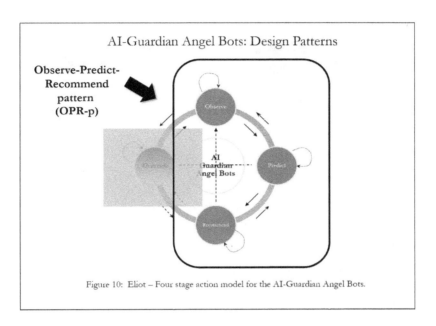

Figure 10: Eliot – Four stage action model for the AI-Guardian Angel Bots.

There are lots of other potential variations of the patterns that can be derived from this model. I wanted to include this last one, so as to show that the pattern can involve three of the stages, rather than only one or two of the stages.

In this design pattern, we have shown that the Observe leads to the Predict which leads to the Recommend, and for which there might not be any need to invoke an override. In which case, the Recommend loops directly up to the Observe, since it has no need for the moment to loop over to the Override.

INITIAL CORE SET OF DESIGN PATTERNS

We have covered nine design patterns. They are listed as a set in the Figure 11 below.

AI-Guardian Angel Bots: Design Patterns

Ref	Pattern Name	Description
DP1	O-p	Observations pattern
DP2	OP-p	Observations-Prediction pattern
DP3	P-p	Predictions pattern
DP4	PR-p	Predictions-Recommends pattern
DP5	R-p	Recommends pattern
DP6	ROV-p	Recommends-Override pattern
DP7	OV-p	Override pattern
DP8	OVO-p	Override-Observations pattern
DP9	OPR-p	Observations-Predictions-Recommends pattern

Figure 11: Eliot – Key design patterns of the four-stage model.

It is likely that nearly all AI Guardian Angel bots would be making use of these design patterns. The specifics of how these would be instantiated will vary depending upon the programming language and tools used to implement them.

These design patterns also apply to the Deep AI side. We have provided for API's that allow for the Deep AI to communicate with the AI Guardian Angel bot, doing so as the "aggressor" that initiates a dialogue. As such, these same design patterns would apply to the Deep AI side, when appropriate and warranted.

There are many other design patterns that can be conceived of. I have provided just a starter set here.

CONCLUSION

Lance B. Eliot

CONCLUSION

You have now read about an emerging area of new technology, AI Guardian Angel bots. What will you do next? I hope that something I've indicated will spark you to action.

Perhaps you'll contribute to the field and start a business to develop and field AI Guardian Angel bots. Maybe you'll focus your next research project on the topic. Or, if you are an existing AI company or high-tech firm adopting Deep AI, I hope that you'll consider the facets identified here about the pending Deep AI trust crisis and do something tangible and constructive about it.

Deep AI has great promise. The potential of a grand setback to advances in developing intelligent automated systems is looming. I am not an alarmist. I am a realist. We all need to make sure that the safety of AI systems gets its due attention, earlier rather than later.

Let me close by quoting a famous Latin phrase: *Forest fortuna adiuvat* (from the Latin; good fortune favors the brave). Please be so!

APPENDIX

APPENDIX A
TEACHING WITH THIS MATERIAL

The material in this book can be readily used either as a supplemental to other content for a class, or it can also be used as a core set of textbook material for a specialized class. Classes where this material is most likely used include any classes at the college or university level that want to augment the class by offering thought provoking and educational essays about AI.

In particular, here are some aspects for class use:

o   Computer Science. Studying Deep AI and/or Bots.

o   Business. Exploring technology and it adoption for business.

o   Sociology. Sociological views on the adoption and advancement of technology.

Specialized classes at the undergraduate and graduate level can also make use of this material.

For each chapter, consider whether you think the chapter provides material relevant to your course topic. There is plenty of opportunity to get the students thinking about the topic and force them to decide whether they agree or disagree with the points offered and positions taken. I would also encourage you to have the students do additional research beyond the chapter material presented (I provide next some suggested assignments they can do).

RESEARCH ASSIGNMENTS ON THESE TOPICS

Your students can find background material on these topics, doing so in various business and technical publications. I list below the top ranked AI related journals. For business publications, I would suggest the usual culprits such as the Harvard Business Review, Forbes, Fortune, WSJ, and the like.

Here are some suggestions of homework or projects that you could assign to students:

a) <u>Assignment for Deep AI topic</u>: Research and prepare a paper and a presentation on a specific aspect of Deep AI, Machine Learning, ANN, etc. The paper should cite at least 3 reputable sources. Compare and contrast to what has been stated in this book.

b) <u>Assignment for the AI Guardian Angel Bot topic</u>: Research and prepare a paper and AI Guardian Angel Bots. Cite at least 3 reputable sources and analyze the characterizations. Compare and contrast to what has been stated in this book.

c) <u>Assignment for a Business topic</u>: Research and prepare a paper and a presentation on businesses and advanced technology. What is hot, and what is not? Cite at least 3 reputable sources. Compare and contrast to the depictions in this book.

d) <u>Assignment to do a Startup</u>: Have the students prepare a paper about how they might startup a business in this realm. They must submit a sound Business Plan for the startup. They could also be asked to present their Business Plan and so should also have a presentation deck to coincide with it.

You can certainly adjust the aforementioned assignments to fit to your particular needs and the class structure. You'll notice that I ask for 3 reputable cited sources for the paper writing based assignments. I usually steer students toward "reputable" publications, since otherwise they will cite some oddball source that has no credentials other than that they happened to write something and post it onto the Internet. You can define "reputable" in whatever way you prefer, for example some faculty think Wikipedia is not reputable while others believe it is reputable and allow students to cite it.

The reason that I usually ask for at least 3 citations is that if the student only does one or two citations they usually settle on whatever they happened to find the fastest. By requiring three citations, it usually seems to force them to look around, explore, and end-up probably finding five or more, and then whittling it down to 3 that they will actually use.

I have not specified the length of their papers, and leave that to you to tell the students what you prefer. For each of those assignments, you could end-up with a short one to two pager, or you could do a dissertation length paper. Base the length on whatever best fits for your class, and the credit amount of the assignment within the context of the other grading metrics you'll be using for the class.

I mention in the assignments that they are to do a paper and prepare a presentation. I usually try to get students to present their work. This is a good practice for what they will do in the business world. Most of the time, they will be required to prepare an analysis and present it. If you don't have the class time or inclination to have the students present, then you can of course cut out the aspect of them putting together a presentation.

If you want to point students toward highly ranked journals in AI, here's a list of the top journals as reported by *various citation counts sources* (this list changes year to year):

o   Communications of the ACM
o   Artificial Intelligence
o   Cognitive Science
o   IEEE Transactions on Pattern Analysis and Machine Intelligence
o   Foundations and Trends in Machine Learning
o   Journal of Memory and Language
o   Cognitive Psychology
o   Neural Networks
o   IEEE Transactions on Neural Networks and Learning Systems
o   IEEE Intelligent Systems
o   Knowledge-based Systems

GUIDE TO USING THE CHAPTERS

For each of the chapters, I provide next some various ways to use the chapter material. You can assign the tasks as individual homework assignments, or the tasks can be used with team projects for the class. You can easily layout a series of assignments, such as indicating that the students are to do item "a" below for say Chapter 1, then "b" for the next chapter of the book, and so on.

a) What is the main point of the chapter and describe in your own words the significance of the topic,

b) Identify at least two aspects in the chapter that you agree with, and support your concurrence by providing at least one other outside researched item as support; make sure to explain your basis for disagreeing with the aspects,

c) Identify at least two aspects in the chapter that you disagree with, and support your disagreement by providing at least one other outside researched item as support; make sure to explain your basis for disagreeing with the aspects,

d) Find an aspect that was not covered in the chapter, doing so by conducting outside research, and then explain how that aspect ties into the chapter and what significance it brings to the topic,

e) Interview a specialist in industry about the topic of the chapter, collect from them their thoughts and opinions, and readdress the chapter by citing your source and how they compared and contrasted to the material,

f) Interview a relevant academic professor or researcher in a college or university about the topic of the chapter, collect from them their thoughts and opinions, and readdress the chapter by citing your source and how they compared and contrasted to the material,

g) Try to update a chapter by finding out the latest on the topic, and ascertain whether the issue or topic has now been solved or whether it is still being addressed, explain what you come up with.

The above are all ways in which you can get the students of your class involved in considering the material of a given chapter. You could mix things up by having one of those above assignments per each week, covering the chapters over the course of the semester or quarter.

As a reminder, here are the chapters of the book and you can select whichever chapters you find most valued for your particular class:

Chapter Title

1	Issues of Trust About Deep AI
2	AI Guardian Angel Bots: Key To AI Trustworthiness
3	API's for Deep AI and AI Guardian Angel Bots
4	Ecosystem of AI Guardian Angel Bots
5	Ratings of AI Guardian Angel Bots
6	Overcoming Deep AI Failure Modes (Robot Cleaning Example)
7	Multiple Agents: Deep AI and AI Guardian Angel Bots
8	Belief Systems of Deep AI and AI Guardian Angel Bots
9	Design Patterns for AI Guardian Angel Bots

I also include on the next pages some of the key diagrams. These are handy tools to be used for teaching purposes.

AI-Guardian Angel Bots: Four Stage Action Model

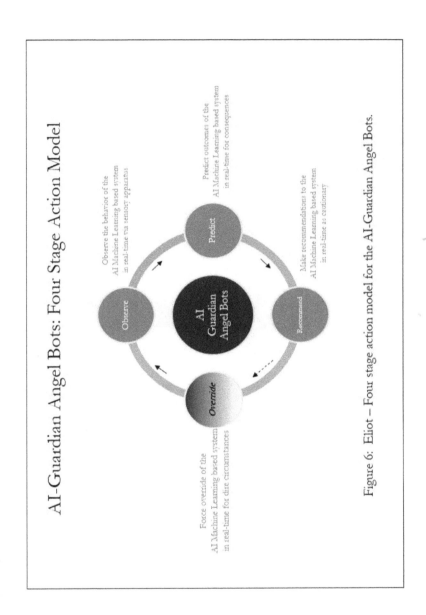

Figure 6: Eliot – Four stage action model for the AI-Guardian Angel Bots.

Lance B. Eliot

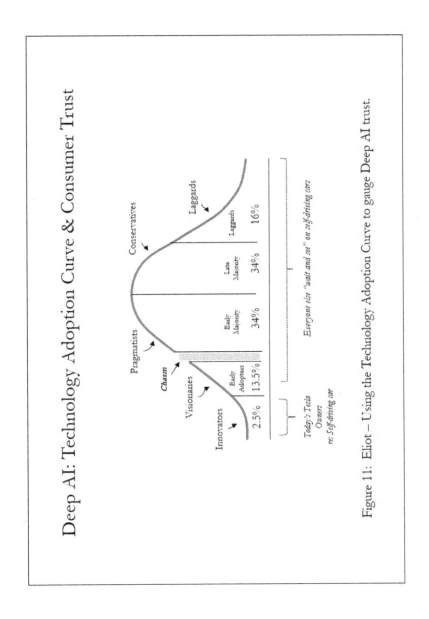

Figure 11: Eliot – Using the Technology Adoption Curve to gauge Deep AI trust.

Lance B. Eliot

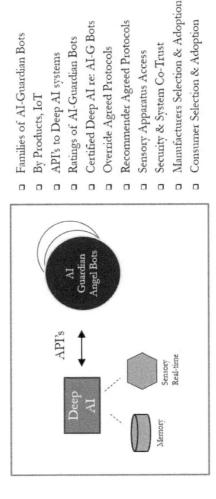

AI-Guardian Angel Bots: Systems Aspects

- Families of AI-Guardian Bots
- By Products, IoT
- API's to Deep AI systems
- Ratings of AI-Guardian Bots
- Certified Deep AI re: AI-G Bots
- Override Agreed Protocols
- Recommender Agreed Protocols
- Sensory Apparatus Access
- Security & System Co-Trust
- Manufacturers Selection & Adoption
- Consumer Selection & Adoption

API's

AI Guardian Angel Bots

Deep AI

Sensory Real-time

Memory

Figure 15: Eliot – Systems aspects for next steps in emergence of AI-Guardian Angel Bots

AI-Guardian Angel Bots: Design Patterns

Ref	Pattern Name	Description
DP1	O-p	Observations pattern
DP2	OP-p	Observations-Prediction pattern
DP3	P-p	Predictions pattern
DP4	PR-p	Predictions-Recommends pattern
DP5	R-p	Recommends pattern
DP6	ROV-p	Recommends-Override pattern
DP7	OV-p	Override pattern
DP8	OVO-p	Override-Observations pattern
DP9	OPR-p	Observations-Predictions-Recommends pattern

Figure 11: Eliot – Key design patterns of the four-stage model.

ABOUT THE AUTHOR

Dr. Lance B. Eliot, MBA, PhD is the CEO of Techbruim, Inc., and has over twenty years of industry experience including serving as a corporate officer in a billion dollar firm and was a Partner in a major executive services firm. He is also a serial entrepreneur having founded, ran, and sold several high-tech related businesses. He previously hosted the popular radio show *Technotrends* that was also available on American Airlines flights via their in-flight audio program. Author or co-author of six books and over 300 articles, he has made appearances on CNN, and has been a frequent speaker at industry conferences.

A former professor at the University of Southern California (USC), he founded and led an innovative research lab on Artificial Intelligence in Business. Known as the "AI Insider" his column on AI advances and trends was widely read and cited. He also previously served on the faculty of the University of California Los Angeles (UCLA), and was a visiting professor at other major universities. He was elected to the International Board of the Society for Information Management (SIM), a prestigious association of over 3,000 high-tech executives worldwide.

He has performed extensive community service, including serving as Senior Science Adviser to the Vice Chair of the Congressional Committee on Science & Technology. He has served on the Board of the OC Science & Engineering Fair (OCSEF), where he is also has been a Grand Sweepstakes judge, and likewise served as a judge for the Intel International SEF (ISEF). He served as the Vice Chair of the Association for Computing Machinery (ACM) Chapter, a prestigious association of computer scientists. Dr. Eliot has been a shark tank judge for the USC Mark Stevens Center for Innovation on start-up pitch competitions, and served as a mentor for several incubators and accelerators in Silicon Valley and Silicon Beach. He serves on several Boards and Committees at USC, including the Marshall Alumni Association (MAA) Board for Los Angeles and Orange County in Southern California.

Dr. Eliot holds a PhD from USC, MBA, and Bachelor's in Computer Science, and earned the CDP, CCP, CSP, CDE, and CISA certifications. Born and raised in Southern California, and having traveled and lived internationally, he enjoys scuba diving, surfing, and sailing.

ADDENDUM

AI Guardian Angel Bots for Deep AI Trustworthiness

Practical Advances in Artificial Intelligence (AI) and Machine Learning

By
Dr. Lance B. Eliot, MBA, PhD

———

For supplemental materials of this book, visit:

www.lance-blog.com

For special orders of this book, contact:

LBE Press Publishing

Email: LBE.Press.Publishing@gmail.com

www.ingramcontent.com/pod-product-compliance
Lightning Source LLC
Chambersburg PA
CBHW051236050326
40689CB00007B/937